Advance Praise

"Dr. Karyne Messina's latest book, *Barbie and the Great American Identity Crisis: The Unfortunate Reality of a Nation Plagued by Racism, Patriarchy, and Stark Hypocrisy*, is a brilliant analysis of contemporary American life that examines the consequences of identity theft as a psychoanalytic event. She capitalizes on the current Barbie zeitgeist by making comparisons between the iconic Barbie doll, 'Barbie,' the 2023 major motion picture, and what many Americans are experiencing in their lives right now: unexplained feelings of loneliness and despair.

Erosion of personal identity leaves individuals adrift and devoid of purpose and direction, and by way of parallel, Dr. Messina exposes Barbie's past as the German doll Lilli and her subsequent transformation into a global commodity by Mattel.

Central here is the disillusionment permeating society stemming from the loss of identity. Using Erik Erikson's stages of development as her framework, Dr. Messina explains the precariousness of identity formation and its relationship to social isolation. Without a firm sense of self, she argues, people are likely to drift into isolation. The consequences of this society-wide are sobering.

Barbie and the Great American Identity Crisis serves as a poignant wake-up call, urging readers to confront the realities of identity loss.

I wholeheartedly recommend this book to anyone who wishes to confront the reality of identity loss and the destructive nature of losing one's sense of identity."

—Harry Gill, MD, PhD, Medical Director, Embark
Cabin John, Medical Director, Clinical Assistant Professor
of Psychiatry, George Washington University

"It's intriguing—I could not put it down.

If you left the movie *Barbie* thinking profoundly about the doll's impact on women, as well as sexism, misogyny, and patriarchy—then you will enjoy *Barbie and the Great American Identity Crisis: The unfortunate reality of a nation plagued by racism, patriarchy, and stark hypocrisy* by Dr. Karyne Messina. The book does a deep dive into the issues broached in the film, including how, like Barbie, Americans are having intense identity crises and how it's affecting the world. Referencing historical events, environmental crises, and other popular movies, Dr. Karyne Messina makes a clear case of how pervasive and damaging patriarchy and dishonest identity crises are to women and men and she creatively puts Barbie on the couch for analytic therapy. She explains how America will continue to suffer from an identity crisis, and repeat the same mistakes (celebration of greed and the cruel exploitation of people, nature, and animals) for selfish reasons until Americans realize they should, as is stated in the book, 'follow the path of truth and accept responsibility for wrongdoing.' I highly recommend this book, which like the Barbie movie, is thought-provoking, educational, and engaging."

—CK Westbrook, environmentalist and science fiction writer who lives and works in Washington, DC. She recently wrote a trilogy called The Impact Series.

"To read the way Karyne Messina's beautiful, complex mind works is to be enriched. She has found a creative way to show what an analysis can achieve in opening an authentic life path, while contrasting crushing social and psychological forces with generative ones. This as she puts an imagined Barbie-as-patient on the couch to illustrate her societal analysis of, among other ills, the harm patriarchy does to women and men alike, how matriarchy is not the answer, and how the answer lies in achieving minds that nourish true equality between the sexes. Throughout she illuminates not only the blockbuster Barbiemovie and the origin story of the Barbie doll, but a broad swath of cinema and scholarship as well.

Through sharing what an analysis did for Barbie in a make-believe world of fantasy, Dr. Messina invites readers to consider what can happen in real life if a person participates with an analyst or analytic therapist in an intensive process that can free one up from inner conflict and lack of purpose. Barbie rediscovered her identity which allowed her to make a major contribution to society as an environmental expert. She also got married and had a child. While Barbie's success occurred in an imaginary world, similar changes occur with regularity when real people participate in psychoanalysis or psychoanalytic psychotherapy.

Dr. Messina, however, doesn't stop there. This deceptively slim volume is a big book, one about identity crisis and the challenges and discomfort involved in regaining or achieving authentic identity. Dr. Messina argues persuasively that Barbie's identity crisis mirrors the one now roiling our nation, and that this identity crisis interferes with solving major problems. In putting the nation on the couch, she nonetheless remains optimistic that we can as a nation take our cues from Barbie and move toward a brighter future."

—Wendy Jacobson, MD, Head, Department of Psychoanalytic Education (DPE) American Psychoanalytic Association, Adjunct Professor of Psychiatry & Behavioral Sciences at Emory University School of Medicine, Training & Supervising Analyst, Emory University Psychoanalytic Institute

"In 1974, the Counseling Center of my then campus Appalachian State University in Boone, NC, placed a life-sized, beautifully colored, poster of the 'old' Barbie in the Student Union. The purpose was obvious: 'Don't fall for this portrayal of a woman's image.' The presentation left such a profound impression that my wife, then a first-year student, vividly recalls the message that contradicted Barbie and some of the women in her family.

This volume carefully explores the many different iterations of Barbie and the doll's impact on, and reflection of, America's hypocritical, male-centric, and white society. It illustrates vividly how girls for several generations, and with them a considerable portion of society, fell into the Barbie trap. This is a well-executed and thoughtful analysis."

—Peter W. Petschauer, PhD, Dr h.c. emeritus professor,
Appalachian State University, author and poe.

"The Barbie doll represented the 1950's WASP notions of a Venus idol. In the 60's the G.I. Joe doll was the ego-ideal of the male, muscular killing machine, a Hercules idol. They are our modern idols, now made of plastic instead of stone. They reinforce the primitive gender ideals that come naturally to immature minds. However, it is the role of parents to socialize children to have a healthy capacity for a mature identity and healthy intimacy. Dr. Messina's book is a brilliant examination of what Barbie says about our collective psychology and what we need to do to improve it. My favorite chapter is when Dr. Messina takes Barbie into psychoanalysis. It is a charming lesson in healing one's identity."

—Robert M. Gordon, Ph.D. ABPP
Board Certified in Clinical Psychology and Psychoanalysis
Website: https://www.mmpi-info.com/
TED Talk: https://youtu.be/R7vP01U8qr4

Barbie and the Great American Identity Crisis

Barbie

and the
Great American
Identity Crisis

The Unfortunate Reality of a Nation Plagued by
Racism, Patriarchy, and Stark Hypocrisy

Dr. Karyne E. Messina

PI Press

Barbie ans the Great American Identity Crisis
PI Press, Chevy Chase, MD

Cover image by dmitri_gromov/stock.adobe.com.
Lili image on page 23 by SSPL/Getty Images.
Barbie image on page 23 by Robyn Beck/AFP via Getty Images.

Book design by Vinnie Kinsella, Paper Chain Book Publishing Services

ISBN 978-1-7362388-1-3 (paperback)
ISBN 978-1-7362388-2-0 (ebook)

Contents

Introduction 1

Essay 1: The Great American Identity Crisis......................................9
How Barbie Exemplifies the Way We Developed Psychologically as a Nation

Essay 2: Clipped Wings..33
Welcome to the Mojo-Dojo Casa House

Essay 3: Barbie on the Couch 51
How Therapy Might Have Changed Her World and Ours; A Snippet of Her Analysis

Essay 4: Barbie's Various Roles 71
Social Media Change Agent, Environmentalist, and AI Specialist

Essay 5: The Original Identity Crisis in America 89
Exploitation Nation Pre-Barbie

Essay 6: The Effects of the American Identity Crisis 101
How Understanding Projective Identification, Mentalization, Reparative Leadership, and How Truth and Reconciliation Commissions Work Could Make a Difference

Conclusion 115

Acknowledgments

I wish to thank Margot Robbie and Greta Gerwig, who helped us all understand what it means to lose one's identity in contemporary America. *Barbie* the blockbuster movie isn't primarily about plastic dolls; it's about what happens when people lose their sense of self and how being forced to don a false identity eventually backfires.

Thank you to Rolf Hausser, the inventor of Lilli, Barbie's predecessor and prototype for Mattel co-founder Ruth Handler. Hausser never received widespread credit for his creation of Lilli. I wish to acknowledge him and apologize for the Mattel corporation's unfair behavior toward him.

I also wish to thank Barbara Richter, my talented researcher, writer, and editor who provides invaluable assistance and wise counsel.

Thank you to the team who helped me publish this book in a timely manner: Vinnie Kinsella of Paper Chain Book Publishing Services, Maria Carola, my literary publicist, and John Knecht, my superb proofreader.

Finally, I would like to thank the members of my family who are part of the "Pink Shirt Barbie Crusaders" who enlightened me about various aspects of this "more than meets the eye" movie, including Ayla, Christopher, Olivia, Isabel, Kiki, Ann, and Gary.

Introduction

On a train to New Jersey in January of 2024, I recalled my first trip as a five-year-old child on the same route. This time, I was going to a funeral with my daughter. The last time I was on this route, I was blissfully romping around having fun with my mother and the friendly people in the dining car. They seemed delighted to see a carefree child who was excited about her first big trip. In my secure world, life was filled with adventure around every bend in the tracks. I was living at a time when I felt safe.

America is a different place now. Crime is rampant, school shootings are commonplace, and the upcoming presidential election strikes fear in the hearts of many who believe democracy as we know it may become a thing of the past.

Who would have thought that was a possibility during my first train ride as a child? How have we changed so much as a nation? Why is our country so divided? I believe part of the answer lies in our lost identity. We can no longer answer questions about our country we thought we knew so well in the past: *Who are Americans? What do we stand for? Is truth still important? Do we care about our fellow citizens, or are we living in a "dog eat dog" world where people are only out for themselves? What happened to our sense of community where our neighbors mattered?* I am not trying to sound nostalgic—these are questions rooted in psychoanalytical thought. A loss of identity has much greater implications than a yearning for times gone by; it can lead to the destabilization of an entire nation. And yes, Barbie had a role in that identity crisis and, I believe, can help forge a better future.

In *Barbie and the Great American Identity Crisis: The Unfortunate Reality of a Nation Plagued by Racism, Patriarchy, and Stark Hypocrisy,* I attempt to answer some of these questions while suggesting ways we might repair at least some of the damage done by our neoliberal ways of living and perhaps regaining the integrity we once had or at least thought we had.

The development or loss of an identity, whether experienced by a person or a nation, is one of the stages of development formulated by psychoanalyst Eric Erikson. Consider the case of Barbie, who was actually Lilli before her identity was stolen from her and the German toymaker who created her. How did that happen is America in the 1950s? At a time of "innocence" before neoliberalism emerged in America, we learned how to comport ourselves. We were also taught to be truthful and to stand up for what we believed in.

This idea led me to wonder whether anyone knew what was happening at Mattel. Were people aware that taking a product from another company was wrong? I suspect the answer might be "yes" since I recall reading something Frederick Douglass said in a speech he gave when the District of Columbia was commemorating the 23rd anniversary of emancipation. The year was 1876 when he said to the crowd that was observing the ceremony, "The life of the nation is secure only while the nation is honest, truthful and virtuous." If the essence of integrity was known in the 19th century, it was certainly known 75 years later in the 20th century.

How do we define our country's identity now? Have we moved away from the proverbial land of the free? Can children feel as carefree as I once did? These are some of the questions I attempt to answer in the essays of this book.

In the first essay, readers learn what it means to experience an existential identity crisis as seen through the experience of Stereotypical Barbie from Greta Gerwig's blockbuster hit. Though she is a doll who one day wakes up with flat feet, Barbie's experiences mirror what we are going through as a nation. (You'll see—just read it.) Essay One also describes how Ruth Handler employed certain defensive maneuvers to justify snatching Barbie from the German toymaker mentioned above while claiming the riches and accolades for herself and Mattel. Handler's actions left the true creator of Lilli heartbroken and destitute. The Mattel corporation is now a billion dollar company while the German toy company went out of business years ago.

Handler and Mattel got diversity all wrong as well. While Mattel finally made a Black Barbie in 1980, children from all racial backgrounds still prefer the white, blonde Barbie. Why? We'll explore that as well in the first part of the book.

The manosphere is also discussed in the first essay, where projective identification comes into play as hypermasculinity rears its ugly head: Those recognizing in themselves stereotypically feminine qualities as well as those who assume failure in achieving socially idealized masculinity project their self-hatred onto women. These situations never work out well.

The second essay is about Ken and how, in the *Barbie* movie, he is put down by the Barbies since he is only seen as arm candy. The Kens are the objectified class in Barbie Land. However, the Kens get to work taking over Barbie Land after they learn about patriarchy. A malfunctioning matriarchy caused this imbalance, which suggests that a full-throttle matriarchy is hazardous to equality between the sexes.

The Kens experience an existential crisis after being tricked by the Barbies into losing their power. In this essay, a short review of three movies helps to depict the dilemma men and women face while maintaining that delicate balance of power in our decidedly patriarchal society. In *American Beauty* and *Madea's Family Reunion*, women are depicted as either victims who are exploited or as props for men to use to promote misogyny and patriarchy under the guise of matriarchy.

In essay three, Barbie is transformed into a person in order to participate in her therapy, something she desperately needed after having many struggles in life that emanated from her lack of knowing herself because her identity was taken from her by the Handlers and Mattel.

In this fantasy analysis, Barbie calls me to inquire about my availability after having been referred to me by one of my former patients who moved from the D.C.-Metro area to California. I agree to see her for a consultation. After meeting with her for four sessions, I begin an analysis with her.

I initially hesitated because I wasn't sure how well she would be able to express her anger since she had been compliant from the time the Handlers took her from her homeland when she was an impressionable young woman. Unlike most girls her age, she never made a statement about who she was as a person since becoming Barbie. However, as I learned more about her, I came to know that she was initially Lilli, a spunky, sassy young woman from Germany. This gave me hope that we could together find the real person that had been posing as someone else for approximately 30 years.

In the fourth essay, the fruits of Barbie's labor in her analysis are realized as she enters the real world. After attending graduate school where she received a degree in Environmental Intelligence, she initially became a reporter assigned to investigate companies who violated environmental standards. While she was very committed to her work, her outlook about climate change wasn't as bleak as many of her co-workers and fellow advocates who work in the field. Her philosophy seemed similar to Heather White's ideas that are stated in her book, *One Green Thing*. From their perspectives, individuals can still make a difference by contributing to at least one thing to save our planet from disastrous consequences.

Barbie also believes, as does White, that we have the technology to prevent an environmental calamity. What we need to figure out is how to collaborate to save our planet. We can only do that through active listening in an atmosphere of mutual respect. Barbie learned the hard way that you can only force people to do things for a little while. Eventually, they revolt. To save the planet, everyone needs to have a voice because everyone deserves to be heard. Disagreement should not be discouraged since no particular person or group has all of the right answers. However, a respectful atmosphere needs to be created in order for progress to be made.

Essay five tells the reader how the initial European settlers and their offspring employed a type of projection like Melanie Klein's projective identification by placing negative aspects of themselves or their negative characteristics onto others. In what I believe was one of the greatest genocides in recent history, European settlers nearly wiped out people who had successfully lived in North America for thousands of years. While we cast aspersions on other countries who attempt to wipe out other people in their own countries or continents, our ancestors are guilty of the same crime.

The last essay offers ideas for how people can repair the damage they have done. It includes taking responsibility for their own negative thoughts, behaviors, and qualities that they have unconsciously evacuated from their minds while attributing them to others. This is the process that occurs in *projective identification.* Fundamentally this means that people need to take responsibility for their own negative ways of being that they have historically attributed to others. I have called this the "taking back of projections."

Mentalization is a helpful concept to those trying to repair relationships. Unfortunately, few people, including professionals, understand its importance and how to implement it. It essentially means being able to recognize one's feelings and thoughts as well as recognizing and respecting the thoughts and feelings of others. If this process is not developed and nurtured in childhood, it can be learned in adulthood. It is essential if people are able to have meaningful relationships with others. This idea does not imply people have to come to an agreement, but instead it is imperative for each person to respect that the other person has a right to his or her own opinion. This same idea applies to groups of people.

One way to conceptualize this process is to think about Melanie Klein's paranoid-schizoid and depressive positions. In the first position, people don't take responsibility for their own actions and instead project unwanted aspects of themselves or their group onto others. In the depressive position, when people are able to "take back their projections," that which has been blamed on someone else or another group is now "owned" in a new way.

While this is an onerous undertaking, the "taking back of projections" can be achieved with the right kind of leaders. When massive aggression is absorbed by a leader who can metabolize these feelings and "give them back" in a more palatable manner, change can occur.

Truth and Reconciliation has also been an effective way for warring groups to come together after many years of acrimony and outright warfare. It is a difficult process and is only truly effective when all parties who were involved in suppressing others agree to participate in the process. Given the paucity of examples, you can imagine how often groups are willing to engage in an undertaking of this type.

The most well-known example of a Truth and Reconciliation Council (TRC) was organized by Nelson Mandela in South Africa. While it has been successful to an extent, there have been some limitations because all of the offending parties did not agree to participate. However, the public was involved in uncovering the truth about the human rights violations that took place during Apartheid when the Dutch ran the country.

Another example of the implementation of reparative leadership and truth and reconciliation occurred after the Rwandan genocide in 1994 when country leaders adopted part of the South African model. In this example, the right kind of leaders helped the Hutus and the Tutsis reconcile. This was a difficult task since both groups were filled with anger and rage at members of the other tribe who previously had been their neighbors and part of their community. Killings and retribution made blame, finger-pointing and hatred most challenging to untangle. In this process, a shift from the paranoid-schizoid position to the depressive position occurred. This made it possible for former enemies to repair their relationships that had been severely damaged.

While we face different challenges—reclaiming an identity is not easy—if Barbie (as seen in the movie) can make the leap from a plastic plaything with eternal "life" to a human who will grow old and die, then I am optimistic that we can take our cues from her and move forward toward a brighter future.

Essay One

The Great American Identity Crisis

*How Barbie Exemplifies the Way We Developed
Psychologically as a Nation*

Truth is powerful and it prevails.
—SOJOURNER TRUTH

*Somewhere along the way I feel as though I lost my identity
and it's not like losing a passport, it feels more like losing
someone so dear to your heart that it pains you every day
to be so unsure if you'll ever see them again or not.*
—DONAL O'CALLAGHAN

*Yes, Barbie changed everything. Then, she
changed it all again.…Because Barbie can
be anything, women can be anything.*
—*BARBIE*, the movie (2023)

In Greta Gerwig's 2023 blockbuster movie *Barbie*, the titular protagonist experiences an existential identity crisis. For the residents of Barbie Land—stereotypical Barbie and her Barbie cohort—everything is always perfect. Plus, each Barbie knows precisely what her role is in this magical place: There's President Barbie, Lawyer Barbie, Dr. Barbie, and even Proust Barbie, and all work harmoniously for the betterment of other Barbies. The Kens are an afterthought, but even they know their place—they are beautiful appendages who live and die by the Barbies.

Life was grand until, one day, Stereotypical Barbie wakes up to flat feet, followed by cellulite, bad breath, and thoughts of death. At first, she thinks she's "malfunctioning," but it becomes clear that Stereotypical Barbie is having an identity crisis. Her initial mission is to find the human in the real world who is playing with her and having sad thoughts, but that morphs into a larger mission of self-discovery. *Who is Barbie?* Does it matter if Barbie has an identity or not? And does her lack of self-understanding reflect anything about Americans today? I believe the answer is yes. This movie is a fanciful representation of what many Americans are experiencing now—a full-on identity crisis—and if we don't discover who we are and what we're here for, many of us are in for a severe mental collapse that could easily lead to further breakdowns in society and social relationships. Decision making, resilience, and courage under fire are all touched in some way or another by a person's sense of self.

America is in the grip of an identity crisis, one that is causing people to lose their sense of themselves as individuals, as members of their communities, and as citizens of a democratic nation.

Social media as a technological tool is exacerbating the crisis because of the negative ways in which information is shared and consumed, a phenomenon that is determining who we like, what we wear, and how we think about the world.

To make matters worse, our collective identity crisis is causing a kind of stasis, an inertia that renders us incapable of making tangible gains toward tackling, among other issues, the growing threat of authoritarianism around the world as well as the worsening climate crisis. *Why bother fixing things? If I don't know who I am, why bother trying to make things better for someone else? I might as well just ride things out.* People who had hoped to have children are rethinking their decision because they don't want to bring offspring into a world they think will be uninhabitable.

Identity is a powerful force that shapes our beliefs, values, and behaviors. When a community's identity is threatened, people may become defensive and resistant to change. When experiencing identity crises, people cannot easily build consensus on how to address anything, such as the climate emergency or rampant community violence. In fragile or compromised mental states, people may understandably be more focused on protecting their own interests versus the common good, but this inward-only focus can, in turn, lead to political gridlock and inaction.

A sort of ennui has crept into our collective consciousness: *I don't know who I am anymore, and I don't think it matters, either.*

How did we get here? And what does Barbie have to do with any of it?

To determine how we wound up in this psychological impasse, I propose examining an era when some Americans (mostly white, heterosexual, and middle class) enjoyed life within defined social structures—the 1950s. I am using this era only as a reference point and not as an ideal—I do not believe that the way to fix our current predicament is to revert to gender-conforming stereotypes and raging patriarchy—but I believe we can gain helpful insights into our psychological makeup by examining how middle-class (implicitly white) Americans and American media perceived themselves. While there were a myriad of inequities, people seemed to understand themselves and where they stood in society. It has been argued that the 1950s was a "golden era" for middle-class Americans and the American Dream (Brinkley, 2012).

The 1950s were also a time when German psychologist and psychoanalyst Erik Erikson formulated his hypotheses about the eight stages of development that start in infancy and continue through adulthood. Erikson determined that for people to live happy and emotionally centered lives, they need to master certain developmental milestones at each stage.

Erikson's theory of psychosocial development provides a framework for understanding how individuals form their identities throughout their lives. His fifth stage of development, known as "Identity versus Identity Confusion," is particularly relevant to the experience of white middle-class Americans in the 1950s. During this developmental stage, the goal is to develop a strong and positive sense of self, anchored in values, beliefs, and goals. The social and economic conditions of the 1950s provided a supportive environment for many white middle-class Americans to achieve this sense of identity. The prevailing cultural norms, the emphasis on conformity, and the promise of the American Dream reinforced a sense of belonging.

Barbie came into existence during this relatively stable moment in American history. Ruth Handler, her alleged creator (I will explain why I use the term "alleged" later), said that her philosophy regarding Barbie revolved around the notion that "the little girl could be anything she wanted to be. Barbie always represented the fact that a woman has choices." Mattel solidified this idea in their marketing when they made the saying official in 1985: "You can be anything."[1]

And yet, despite this open-ended invitation to be anyone or do anything, Americans have endured a decades-long identity crisis. We face a complex psychological crisis characterized by confusion, uncertainty, and fragmentation exacerbated by several other factors, including rapid social change, economic inequality, political polarization, and technological advancement, all of which can lead to disorientation, displacement, resentment, and alienation. The concept of Barbie also has contributed to this problem that is afflicting many Americans by promoting an unrealistic body image, perpetuating gender stereotypes, and undermining diversity, all while contributing to consumerism as well as a focus on external validation rather than intrinsic self-worth.

---

1. A toy maker for a German company and a Mattel vice president both claimed they were the actual creators of Barbie (Breznican, 2023).

Of course, Barbie is not the sole cause of the psychological crisis of identity afflicting Americans. Still, she symbolizes the cultural forces that have contributed to this crisis. By critically examining Barbie and her place in society, we can begin to understand the roots of this crisis and perhaps take steps to address it.

BARBIE'S UNREALISTIC BODY STANDARDS

Using the original body molds from the 1950s as a reference, if Barbie were a human, she would likely need a wheelchair to get around: At seven feet, two inches, 100 pounds, and with bust-waist-hips measurements of 36-18-33, Barbie would probably be unable to support her body weight. Multiple studies indicate that playing with ultra-thin dolls with unrealistic shapes can hurt young girls. In 2016, the journal *Body Image* provided research suggesting that girls between six and eight years old cannot shake negative self-perceptions after playing with Barbie and other dolls endowed with unrealistic, ultra-thin shapes. Returning to asexualized dolls such as Dora and Lottie didn't alter the girls' negative perceptions about the ideal shape. As early as age six, girls regarded unattainably thin body types as the ideal, and the data points to Barbie as the conduit for those feelings (Jellinek et al., 2016).

Unless there is early and sustained intervention—studies have shown that playing with normal-sized dolls reinforces positive self-image—this early identification with an ultra-thin ideal seems to contribute to a long-term struggle with depression and eating disorders. It seems as though Handler's idea about the positive things her doll could do for girls was way off base. Instead of helping girls feel invincible, is it possible that these Barbie dolls led girls to feel confused or depressed, as the results published in *Body Image* suggest? Could the emergence of Barbie have stymied their ability to figure out their identity? Rather than inspire girls, Barbie pointed out girls' perceived flaws instead. *Barbies never get acne or frizzy hair—how unfair! If only I could be like Barbie, then everything would be okay.*

These girls carry these warped sensibilities into adulthood, where their fractured identities lead to disorientation and a negative sense of self-worth. Multiply these little girls by the millions, and it's easy to see that we've got more than just a few little girls who don't like themselves; we've got a full-on collective crisis.

IDENTIFICATION: A PROCESS THAT BEGINS EARLY AND LASTS A LIFETIME

Identification with another person begins in infancy when children take in or psychologically absorb various characteristics of their parents. This is part of typical personality development and character formation.[2] While this process continues throughout life, the critical formation period is between the ages of twelve and eighteen, when adolescents explore who they are, what they want to do in life, and what matters to them. For young people across socio-economic and ethnic groups, peer influences—the influence of a teenager's friends rather than parents—increase linearly until about age eighteen (Steinberg & Monahan, 2007). If a young person has a strong sense of self—equipped, essentially, with a well-developed identity as defined by Erikson—such an adolescent is less likely to fall victim to "role confusion," which can lead to depression and even suicidal ideation.

According to Erikson's long-accepted hypotheses, young people in this general age range need *people* with whom they can interact in order

---

2. Freud wrote about identification in 1921 when describing the way babies learn about themselves. This is a process through which an infant develops a sense of self by internalizing the characteristics and behaviors of its caregiver. This process of identification can also be used as a defense maneuver that comes into play to ward off anxiety or seek approval from others.

to identify with them. And though most teenagers outgrow playing with Barbie before they hit puberty, those dolls can cause stunted and underdeveloped psychological growth. No matter how you dress them up, plastic dolls can never replace observing women *actually doing things*. Developing a meaningful connection or mentorship with women living inspirational lives is the most optimal way for young people to develop a positive sense of self. You can't develop an identity and "become anyone you want to be" by playing with plastic dolls.

Suggesting that young girls can project their innermost hopes and desires onto a doll can do a great deal of damage; girls playing with adult-looking dolls are too young to have had enough experience with real women in a multitude of professions to project much of anything other than perhaps a desire to dress Barbie up in fun clothes.

This is particularly true of children who grow up far away from the places Barbie lives, like Malibu. (The internet has shrunk our world, certainly, but our lived reality and our digital one are not always one and the same.) You can't fully know something you haven't experienced. Most Barbies have historically been white, but Americans aren't just white people from middle- and upper-class families. Other dolls were eventually introduced in the 1980s, but for over 20 years, Ruth Handler's dolls were primarily for white children and young adolescents.

In her book *Forever Barbie: The Unauthorized Biography of a Living Doll*, M.G. Lord argues that Barbie is the most potent icon of American culture to emerge from the late 20th century and is "something upon which little girls project their idealized selves." Note the use of the descriptor *something* rather than *someone*.

Projecting an ideal self onto plastic dolls is not how girls and adolescents develop an identity. They must be able to relate to real women, whether that's by watching television programs and plays or attending concerts starring women like Beyoncé or Taylor Swift.

Hence, whatever intention Handler had was not based on an understanding of human development. It may have led to the other side of

Erikson's developmental task, which is *identity diffusion* or *role confusion*. In this state, young people, or people of any age who have never mastered this task earlier in life, feel lost and have little sense of who they are. They often have one relationship after the other and lack stability in their work. Moving from job to job is not unusual when someone does not have a strong sense of identity.

Even if older children and adolescents could turn to Barbie for identity inspiration, the results would be problematic. Barbie could easily cause a great deal of harm, because this formula could only benefit white middle- and upper-class children. In other words, we need experiences with older, wiser people to form our identities. Displaced identities and identity confusion resulting from too much time with Barbie lines up with Erikson's hypothesis that people can't really "know" themselves until they form interactions with others, especially with promising partners in work and love. This process of self-discovery involves selective affirmation and the repudiation of childhood experiences. Identity confusion can occur when this process is disrupted and can lead to pathological regression (Erikson, 1998).

Barbie's inability to know herself in the movie *Barbie* may be why her relationship with Ken was fraught with ambivalence. She does not know who she is as a person, so true intimacy can never be achieved. Instead of evolving into a mature adult, she goes from one friendship to another and belittles Ken—most often without even realizing she's doing it. Although Barbie doesn't trash him on social media as mean girls frequently do these days, she makes fun of him, talks behind his back, excludes him from various events, and is generally unkind to him. Whether or not he deserves this treatment at times is not the point. What is significant is Barbie's inability to engage in an adult, intimate relationship, instead acting as one might expect an adolescent girl to treat a teenage boy.

PROJECTION AND PROJECTIVE IDENTIFICATION

For many years, my work has centered around projection and projective identification. Though sometimes benign, projection is the process wherein people attribute to other people characteristics that belong to them. Projective identification is more destructive and is the way individuals relieve themselves of self-hatred and other intolerable feelings. By projecting their negative characteristics and behaviors onto another or others while believing the recipient is the one with the undesirable quality, trait, or belief they "dispose" of intolerable aspects of themselves in an unconscious process.

The relevance of these mental maneuvers becomes apparent when considering both unconscious and conscious mechanisms employed when forming one's identity. In the case of Ruth Handler, she appeared to need to project her belief onto young girls that "Barbie was born out of a desire to give girls something more…that through the doll, the little girl could be anything she wanted to be" (Kennedy, 2023).

While a private wish is okay, this was not what occurred in Handler's case. The recipients of Handler's projections—young girls, teenagers, and their mothers—took in and started to believe what she said. They believed the Barbie phenomenon was a good thing. They literally and figuratively bought what she (and later Mattel) had to sell. Was Handler's seemingly altruistic act to inspire girls nothing more than a money grab?

RUTH HANDLER GOT DIVERSITY WRONG FROM THE BEGINNING. SO DID MATTEL.

Handler fashioned Barbie as a whiter version of Bild Lilli (the original German doll), and Mattel didn't introduce a lack Barbie until 1980. Although Barbie had friends with darker skin (like Francie, who debuted in 1967), it wasn't until Black people became more affluent that a black Barbie appeared on the American doll scene. While her release appeared to be a moment of progress in the toy industry, some, academics have argued that black Barbie would never have existed if Black Americans hadn't already experienced upward economic and social mobility (Jeffrey, 2023).

While it may have appeared as though this was a significant step forward, had Mattel actually become more enlightened? Did the company care more about the self-concepts of Black children? Or was Mattel only focused on the bottom line? I would think the latter was more likely since American companies tend to follow trends that lead to making the most money possible. Corporations in America optimize profits by following and capitalizing on societal trends. And the introduction of a Black Barbie was no different.

ONE MOTHER'S STORY ABOUT THE EFFECTS OF RACISM

According to one mother, whose story may represent millions of others, after resisting the Barbie craze, she began to buy Barbies for her four-year-old because her little girl kept asking for them. This mother would buy a variety of Barbies, yet her daughter said she didn't want to play with the dark-skinned ones. The mother attributed this to living in what she called "Trump country," where diversity was near impossible. As a white mother, this woman wanted to teach her daughter that being kind and capable of achieving important things shouldn't be limited by skin color (Ashley, 2019).

Mattel seemed on board with this as well by helping close what it calls "the dream gap" (the ability for girls to reach their full potential) for girls starting around five years of age. This makes good promotional copy, but, according to Erikson, the task they have identified is not exactly on target. While there is overlap between each phase of development, the major goal to be achieved during the latency years is Industry versus Inferiority. The focus is on school achievement, not on gender issues. As five-year-olds, children must master new skills and gain competence in various activities. Children who receive encouragement and support for their efforts build a strong sense of industry and accomplishment. However, children who experience limited success or lack encouragement may develop a sense of inferiority.

MATTEL'S NEW BARBIES: DO GIRLS WANT THEM?

Mattel's commitment to diversity and female empowerment is more about lip service and PR than anything else. It wasn't until 2016 that Mattel introduced the supposedly groundbreaking *Fashionistas* line of dolls, which included three new body shapes, seven different skin tones, and multiple new hair shades, eye colors, and facial features. But the blue-eyed blond remains the predominant Barbie on the store shelves. (Ashley, 2019).

Even after Mattel committed to producing more diverse dolls, the company didn't make good on their promise. Many of the professional Barbies are white, including the farmer, the pizza-maker, the teacher, and others. Indeed, there's nothing stopping anyone from buying a Black Barbie doll and dressing her in an outfit of one's choice, but it appears to be clear that the Black doll is the alternative and not the standard.

Body size also influences girls' self-identity and self-esteem. In an experiment in the UK, girls who played with ultra-thin and adult-looking dolls seemed to prefer them. Once given a realistic doll, the effect of the previous play could not be undone. This suggests that it is better to give girls dolls to play with that look more like actual children versus those that resemble adults (Fagan, 2021).

MISOGYNY AND BARBIE: DID A "PERFECT" WOMAN CONTRIBUTE TO A PATRIARCHAL WORLD?

When it comes to a comprehensive analysis of the misogynist groups that have proliferated on a variety of websites, blogs, fora, and social media platforms in a backlash to feminist advances as well as the emergent recognition of gender difference, it is important to grapple with how and why this response might have emerged. In this context, it is easy to see how the manosphere, or online groups dominated by toxic masculinity, not only contributes to the political divisiveness characteristic of our contemporary culture, but also to recent rabid rejections of social advances for women. This is illustrated in *Fantasy, Online Misogyny and the Manosphere: Male Bodies of Dis/Inhibition* by Jacob Johanssen (2022), who explains how "dis/inhibition" is connected and harmful not only to biological women, but to all genders possessing feminine traits.

In this case, projective identification comes into play when hypermasculinity rears its ugly head: Those recognizing in themselves stereotypically feminine qualities as well as those who assume failure in achieving socially idealized masculinity project their self-hatred onto women.

The manosphere, Johanssen contends, enables men to construct a realm in which women aren't a threat to their masculinity because they are, simply, excluded—i.e., absent. In these spaces, men can create imaginary realms in which they are dominant and served both maternally and sexually by submissive women. Their internet personae buoy their identification with the powerful fascist who is inherently defined by technological superiority: Imagine the soldier with a machine gun, aircraft, missile, etc. This identification allows them to disassociate from their bodies and/or social positions and re-establish themselves as hypermasculine. The manosphere is also alluring in its ability to simplify a confusing contemporary reality in which men segment themselves into the nurturing family member and the aggressive participant in capitalism.

Some of these groups and those onto whom they project their unsatisfactory traits deserve mention here.

MANOSPHERE DEFINED

Alt-Right: a group that perpetrates intersectional discrimination (racist, antisemitic, and misogynist)

Incels: an abbreviation for "involuntary celibate," someone who rejects all women based on their self-definition as unable to attract desirable women

MGTOW: Men Going Their Own Way, "a community that advocates a male separatist lifestyle and male supremacy"

NoFap: an anti-porn and anti-masturbation group that is mostly men.

These groups, Johannsen explains, are on forum sites like 4Chan, 8Chan, and Reddit and "play a large part in mainstreaming misogyny" (Johanssen, xxiv).

Johanssen's analysis of the psychological, social, and historical origins of these groups as well as their intersectionality is so thorough and nuanced that it would do a disservice to reduce it in summary. Castration anxiety is one obvious psychoanalytical symptom that is clear to see. However, it is helpful to briefly exemplify some of the attitudes of these men that are as harmful to themselves as they are to those on whom they project their disgust.

The incel community is an example of multiple levels of hatred directed outward and inward. This group has even developed a complex symbolic system that suits their cultish rejection of both men and women who represent what they see as the cause of their own exclusion from society. They term stereotypically attractive men whose physical characteristics and financial success attract women "Chads." The practice of women seeking to "marry up" (for whom prior generations had their own slurs) is called "hypergamy." Incels believe that women are driven by evolution as well as social expectations to improve their status. A "Stacy" is an unintelligent but sexually desirable and promiscuous woman who would never choose them as a partner. As the incels define themselves as socially and physically undesirable, through this reductive categorization, they achieve apathy. Neither a hypergamist nor a Stacy would choose them as a partner, so why try to find one? Better to project their own dissatisfaction onto others, transforming it into despicable characteristics they do not want to believe they could be guilty of themselves.

When projective identification is at play, as it appears to be in many cases involving gender issues, men cast off feelings of self-loathing, weakness, and other negative feelings and project them onto others, mainly women. They thereafter accuse them of being the weak ones. Projective identification is everywhere; there's no escaping it. It is also the case, like it or not, that we live in a patriarchal world.

At the same time, patriarchy is not the natural order of things. From the beginning, babies seek attachment. They enter the world longing for connection. Attachment is what counts to a newborn infant. It's a relational world until love is withdrawn. Patriarchy emerges when a human connection is lost. How do the faces of happy male babies turn into angry faces of men who hate women?

When you put the pieces together, the connection between patrimony and misogyny becomes clearer since patrimony is a *defense* against loss and misogyny, in addition to being another defense, is an offshoot or a manifestation of patriarchy. If we assume that patriarchy comes into being as a result of a loss, then we can assume that misogyny may emerge as a way men toughen up to protect themselves instead of feeling painful emotions. Projective identification is a way of getting rid of the feelings associated with rejection and loss of love. If you can't have love, the next best thing is power.

WHY BARBIE'S LOST IDENTIFY IS IMPORTANT

American girls did not know Barbie was a German sex worker in her previous life. She had a history that started long before 1959 when she made her debut at the New York International Toy Fair. She was not meant to represent the ideal role model who would help young girls dream and imagine what they could be when they grew up. In fact, young German children weren't initially allowed to play with her. Parents considered the doll inappropriate for children. A German brochure from the 1950s described Lilli as "always discreet," and with her impressive wardrobe, she was "the star of every bar." A journalist for *The New Yorker* magazine later referred to Lilli as a "sex doll" (MessyNessy, 2022).

LILLI BECOMES BARBIE

After Handler failed to convince the men at Mattel to create a full-figured woman as a children's doll in 1956, she took her daughter Barbara to Switzerland for a vacation. While there, to their surprise, they found Bild Lilli, a very adult-looking lady doll. Handler bought several of them and copied Lilli with only a few modifications.

The popular (and sanitized) version of Barbie's creation leaves out the fact that Barbie was modeled on a German sex toy. In fact, Lilli began life as a cartoon character in the Hamburg *Bild-Zeitung*, where her primary focus was on sustaining a life of luxury through sex work. Lilli was so popular that the newspaper merchandized her into a profitable and popular gift—for *men* (Monteil, 2023).

Pretending that Barbie was a flawless woman or a blank slate leaves out her history, a classic example of disavowal or a way of projecting—getting rid of—important aspects of the real first female adult doll's personality. In other words, by cancelling Bild Lilli, Handler and Mattel attempted to erase Barbie's past.

Bild Lilli was a sex doll. Her creators envisioned her as such, even if it seems odd and misogynistic that men in the 1950s needed a doll for amusement. It is also possible that we don't know enough about the culture in Germany after WWII, which may have been related to Lilli's creation. No matter what the reason, why hide the truth? It seems like covering up a family secret. Could Barbie have been as influential if it were known that the original full-figured doll was created by a man to entertain other men?

While Barbie was the personification of the perfect American teenager or women celebrated as an icon of Handler's and Mattel's acumen and financial expertise, a German toymaker named Rolf Hausser seethed in a Bavarian village for never receiving any credit for his creation of Bild Lill. Part of Barbie's history includes the tragic story of a bitter old man who could not move on from the events of four decades ago, a man who has been wiped from Barbie's history so thoroughly that only a handful of people in the world know that he was the true creator of Barbie the doll. Except for her skin color (rendered lighter in America) and a few other minor alterations, she and Bild Lilli looked like twins (see images on next page).

Lilli the Germany doll (L) in 1955 and Barbie at her debut in 1959 (R).

MATTEL'S MONETARY GAIN FROM CANCELLING LILLI

There is no Barbie without Lilli. Lilli was a fashionable and sexy woman who went after what she wanted in a cheeky way, much like movie stars from the 1930s and '40s.

It didn't take long for other companies to realize these products' potential, so they were sold in Italy, Scandinavia, and England as "Lilli" or "Lilli Marleen/Marlene." Knock-off dolls were also sold in other countries around the world, such as Hong Kong, France, and Spain (Bullard, 2023).

At this point, Lilli's identity was intact. Then in 1959, at the New York International Toy Show, an 11.5-inch plastic fashion doll made her debut. She had hair with roots like Lilli's hair that was not glued. She also debuted in the same black and white swimsuit and had painted finger- and toenails as well as a head on a swivel and long legs that closed when she sat down. The major difference was her name.

Here we come to an American dilemma. Who do we believe? There's the Ruth Handler story about creating Barbie for all little girls to enjoy, versus taking a German doll she found in Switzerland and pawning it off on Americans as her creation. Which story is true?

And there are still other Barbie origin stories that clash with the official narrative. Jack Ryan, a corporate executive at Mattel, claimed ownership/creatorship of Barbie, as told by Jerry Oppenheimer in his biography (ABC News, 2009).

Ryan's daughter, Ann, also tells a similar story about her father's ownership of Barbie. In her podcast, *Dream House: The Real Story of Jack Ryan*, Ann says her father was not given credit for his patents even though his name is on them, adding that the choice of the name for the doll was her father's since his wife's name was Barbie.

After Ruth Handler's book came out, Jack Ryan had already passed away, so he could not refute anything. Ann told a *New York Post* reporter that Ruth's story was bunk (Oppenheimer, 2023).

Another person who reportedly had a major role in Barbie's success was a psychologist, psychoanalyst, and marketing expert, Ernest Dichter, who was originally from Vienna and was quite knowledgeable about Freud's theories and techniques.

Considered by his contemporaries as a major manipulator, Dichter was an expert at gathering information about all types of products from potential customers and then repackaging what he learned to sell to other consumers. Much of his work was conducted at the Institute of Motivational Research in New York. At this 30-room facility, he placed participants in one area with televisions and unseen observers and tape recorders in other areas. According to Vance Packard, author of *The Hidden Persuaders,* Dichter and his staff of over 20 professionals evaluated participants' responses from their laughs to their sighs (Packard, 1957, pp. 52–53). Based on how participants responded to stimuli, Dichter could predict the types of products they might be likely to buy.

After being hired by Handler because of disappointing initial sales of the first Barbie doll, Dichter told Mattel that they had the wrong marketing approach and claimed they needed to appeal to people's emotions. From his research with focus groups, which he formed with mothers and daughters, he determined that changing the minds of mothers who initially did not like Barbie was of paramount importance because they wanted their daughters to be well-groomed in preparation for marriage.

By finding this vulnerability—a wish for daughters to be married—Handler and Dichter moved Mattel closer to being the most profitable toy company in the world.

This is another illustration of Handler's duplicity. That she merely wanted little girls to be anyone they wished to be through an identification with Barbie seems out of sync with hiring a man whose specialty was to manipulate others to buy a doll that would ultimately prepare them to get married, which was a not-so-subtle message portrayed in the first Barbie television commercial aired in 1959 featuring Barbie's fashion collection, including an exquisite wedding dress.

WHAT HAPPENS WHEN PEOPLE LOSE THEIR IDENTITY

Even when people have established strong identities, they can lose their sense of who they are for a myriad of reasons, including those who have been kidnapped, sex-trafficked victims, some children who are adopted, immigrants, people who are displaced because of war or natural disasters, women who are forced to have a child, and people who aren't allowed to change their gender, among others. Even Barbie had to snuff out all aspects of her Lilli heritage. When this occurs in real life, a false self can emerge, as described by Donald Winnicott, which happens when someone doesn't have access to his or her true self.

WHY BARBIE'S ORIGIN STORY MATTERS

When people lose their sense of self, they lose what matters the most in life. It means they aren't really the people they know themselves to be. Instead, they comply with the wishes of others in order to fit in. Although Winnicott coined the term "false self" in 1960,[3] today, "fear of missing out," or FOMO, captures the essence of this idea. Many people make lifestyle choices based on the desire for external validation, rather than following internal desires and individual preferences. Can this mismatch between desires and reality negatively affect well-being? I believe the answer is a definite "yes."

Loss of identity and the development of a false self affects one's mental health. People who lose their sense of identity or never discovered it in the first place often feel depressed. Quite frequently, nothing matters to them; they feel they have no purpose in life. If the condition is severe, they may suffer a dissociative identify disorder (DID), which means they don't know who they are, sometimes from one minute to the next.

People suffering from a DID don't have one distinct identity. They have two or more totally different personalities wherein their behavior changes with each one. Usually associated with trauma and/or abuse in childhood, the symptoms include loss of memory, feelings of detachment, and feeling as though one is outside of his or her body.

---

3. Winnicott's concept of a false self is rooted in an infant's relationship with his or her mother or primary caregiver who serves as a mirror for the baby while the child learns about the world through what he or she sees on the adult's face. As the child slowly separates psychologically from this primary caregiver, the way she or he adapts to the changes that are part of normal growth and development sets the tone for how a true or false self is formed. If the changes are welcomed, the infant feels real, in which case a true sense of self can develop. If not, a type of altered reality forms wherein the baby develops a false, compliant way of being in the world.

HOW AI COULD IMPACT IDENTITY AND HUMAN CONNECTIONS—MOVING BEYOND BARBIE

In Jeanette Winterson's 2022 book, *12 Bytes: How we Got Here. Where We Might Go Next,* a journey into a fantasy world is explored that may not be something that only exists in the minds of sci-fi aficionados or IT techs. The book explores a new machine culture and the rapidly growing field of sexual robotics wherein real women are being replaced with sex alternatives to sex workers and, by extension, alternatives to women.

These sex dolls can talk, remember past conversations, and be programmed to fit the user's taste. They can be funny, jealous, talkative, shy, or hesitant to the point where her owner can simulate rape.

If this were to happen on a widespread basis, what would this mean for real women? This idea raises the question of whether a new type of lifestyle is emerging. In their 2017 book *The Age of Perversion: Desire and Technology in Psychoanalysis and Culture*, Danielle Knafo and Rocco Lo Bosco discuss how the replacement of people with life-size dolls means that people who develop emotional connections with inanimate objects represent choices one makes versus abnormal behavior (Messina, 2017, p. 1).

While interacting with AI objects may be commonplace in the future, but is it possible to develop authentic connections, especially when you consider Erikson's stages of development, particularly those associated with identity and intimacy? Since the acquisition of an identity and intimacy are human qualities, will AI objects be able to develop these ways of being, or will AI merely convince human beings they share the same ways of relating?

We do not yet know whether these dolls will interact in ways that replicate true human relating between human beings and AI objects, but as I suggested in 2017, the way psychoanalysts interact with "dolls" will certainly change.

While it currently takes the mind of a person to project fantasies onto dolls to make the world of iDollators work, especially if they believe that these inanimate dolls are capable of love, this could change. "In the future, as various devices are imbued with AI, one of the biggest challenges may be for psychoanalysts to interact differently with patients" (Messina, 2020). It also may be the case that AI psychoanalysts may be interacting differently with human beings.

REFERENCES

ABC New. (2009, February 22). *'Toy Monster' details Barbie.* Retrieved February 25, from https://abcnews.go.com/Business/story?id=6934821&page=1

Ashley, S. (2019, May 7). *What Barbie gets wrong about diversity.* Medium. https://medium.com/@Shesreallyfat/barbie-cant-evolve-past-being-a-basic-white-bitch-2785665e2988

Brenner, C. (2002). Conflict, compromise formation, and structural theory. *The Psychoanalytic Quarterly, 71*(3), 397–417. https://doi.org/10.1002/j.2167-4086.2002.tb00519.x

Breznican, A. (2023, July 23). Ruth handler: Sex toys, financial crimes and the origin of barbie. *Vanity Fair.* Retrieved from https://www.vanityfair.com/hollywood/2023/07/ruth-handler-barbie-true-story?redirectURL=%2Fhollywood%2F2023%2F07%2Fruth-handler-barbie-true-story

Brinkley, A. (2012, April 10). *The Gilder Lehrman Institute of American History advanced placement United States history study guide.* The Fifties | AP US History Study Guide from The Gilder Lehrman Institute of American History. https://ap.gilderlehrman.org/history-by-era/fifties/essays/fifties#:~:text=Many%20Americans%20in%20the%201950s,great%20successes%20of%20the%201950s

Bullard, K. (2023, September 12). *The stolen legacy of Bild Lilli.* Hobby Lark. https://hobbylark.com/collecting/The-Stolen-Legacy-Of-Bild-Lilli

Erikson, E. H., & Erikson, J. M. (1998). *The life cycle completed* (p. 82). W. W. Norton & Company. Kindle Edition.

Fagan, A. (2021, March 23). *Barbies may do damage that realistic dolls can't undo.* Psychology Today. https://www.psychologytoday.com/us/blog/beauty-sick/202103/barbies-may-do-damage-realistic-dolls-cant-undo

Jeffrey, J. (2023, July 24). *For generations, black Barbie has been a symbol of power, upward mobility and imagination.* NBCNews.com. https://www.nbcnews.com/news/nbcblk/generations-black-barbie-symbol-power-upward-mobility-playfulness-rcna95927

Jellinek, R. D., Myers, T. A., & Keller, K. L. (2016). The impact of doll style of dress and familiarity on body dissatisfaction in 6- to 8-year-old girls. *Body Image, 18,* 78–85. https://doi.org/10.1016/j.bodyim.2016.05.003

Kennedy, P. (2023, July 26). *The amazing Ruth Handler, the woman behind Barbie.* Antiques Trader. https://www.antiquetrader.com/feature-stories/ruth-handler-the-woman-behind-barbie

Knaffo, D., & Lo Bosco, R. (2017). *The age of perversion: Desire and technology in psychoanalysis and culture.* Routledge.

Lord, M. G. (2004). *Forever Barbie: The unauthorized biography of a real doll.* Walker & Co.

MessyNessy. (2022, December 19). *Meet Lilli, the high-end German call girl who became Barbie.* Messy Nessy Chic. https://www.messynessychic.com/2016/01/29/meet-lilli-the-high-end-german-call-girl-who-became-americas-iconic-barbie-doll/

Monteil, A. (2023a, July 22). *The dark side of Barbie: Crime, racial issues, and rampant sexism.* Rolling Stone. https://www.rollingstone.com/tv-movies/tv-movie-features/barbie-controversies-greta-gerwig-mattel-ruth-handler-sex-doll-sexism-racism-1234792205/

Oppenheimer, J. (2023, July 15). *Battle to be the real Barbie: Toy boss' daughter vs sex-crazed genius' ideal woman*. New York Post. https://nypost.com/2023/07/15/battle-to-be-the-real-barbie-how-two-barbaras-lay-claim-to-inspiring-the-doll-margot-robbie-plays/

Packard, Vance. (1957). *The Hidden Persuaders* (pp. 52-53). Ig Publishing. Kindle Edition

Steinberg, L., & Monahan, K. C. (2007). Age differences in resistance to peer influence. *Developmental Psychology*, *43*(6), 1531–1543. https://doi.org/10.1037/0012-1649.43.6.1531

Essay Two

Clipped Wings

Welcome to the Mojo-Dojo Casa House

> *Say that you are a feminist to most men, and automatically you are seen as the enemy. You risk being seen as a man-hating woman.... Even though not all men are misogynists, feminist thinkers were accurate when we stated that patriarchy in its most basic, unmediated form promotes fear and hatred of females.*
> —Bell Hooks, "Feminist Manhood," *The Will To Change* (2004)

> *Those who do not move, do not notice their chains.*
> —Rosa Luxembourg, Marxist activist (1871–1919)

In the 2023 blockbuster *Barbie*, writer-director Greta Gerwig makes two intertwined arguments: that patriarchy is bad for men and women and that matriarchy is not the appropriate corrective. When "Just Beach Ken" discovers male dominance in the real world, he learns all he can about patriarchy and brings it back to Barbie Land, where he and his fellow Kens rise and refuse to continue to be taken for granted by the Barbies.

In this film fantasy, Barbie Land has been ruled by the ladies since time immemorial—the Barbies hold all leadership positions and excel at everything they do. The Kens are appendages—arm candy, disposable, forgettable. (The Barbies don't even know where the Kens sleep at night.) The Kens are the objectified class in Barbie Land, and the taste of power proves unquenchable, so they make up for lost time. Soon enough, the Kens brainwash the Barbies into believing that their sole reason for existing is to please and pamper the Kens. A malfunctioning matriarchy caused this imbalance, the suggestion being that a full-throttle matriarchy is hazardous to equality between the sexes.

After the brainwashed Barbies are deprogrammed and the Kens are tricked into losing their power, Ken experiences an existential crisis—on par with the one Barbie has been experiencing since her feet went flat in the beginning of the movie: Both characters are trying to figure out who they are and their purpose. As Ken confesses to Barbie, "I just don't know who I am without you… There is no just 'Ken.' That's why I was created. I only exist within the warmth of your gaze. Without it, I'm just another blond guy who can't do flips" (Gerwig, 2023). Eventually, Ken wears a sweatshirt emblazoned with the mantra "I am Kenough," another humorous reversal of gender equality, but this prompts a larger question of men's equality in American patriarchal society. By turns, as a victim of sexism and patriarchy, Ken is representative of American men being left behind in the drive for women's liberation. And when he does realize patriarchy isn't the answer, his initial thought is to return to a matriarchy until Barbie tells him he needs to discover his identity on his own—something many American men never have the privilege to experience.

The past half century of the women's equality movement has been made at men's expense. Contemporary feminism does not want to acknowledge that to create true equality, patriarchy must be dismantled, not to be replaced with matriarchy, but with equality—an equality that values men and allows them to experience the full breadth of human emotions. Failure to do so fails men and fails women by trapping both sexes in a system that only favors a certain type of gender identity, which is hardly a "one size fits all" program.

To create and sustain true gender parity and promote authentic self-identity, the pendulum must not swing in one direction at the expense of another. We have seen what patriarchy does to men and women, and we have also seen the consequences of man-hating feminism. The path forward makes space for both. Achieving equality will require a greater awareness of the consequences wrought by entrenched patriarchal norms that deny men the right to full emotional lives, which, in turn, prevents women from enjoying the same privileges granted to those men who embody the ideal. These stereotypes have been documented extensively in American cinema. We will explore here how men (and, by extension, women) are trapped in a patriarchal existence and how that dynamic is expressed in film.

In *The Will to Change: Men, Masculinity, and Love*, bell hooks examines how contemporary society is fundamentally unfair to women, yes, but also to men. And to create a more just society for women, men must also be freed from the yoke of patriarchy. Men, she argues, are conditioned to hide their feelings unless those feelings express ferocity or anger, thus discouraging men from living to their full potential. Male domination benefits men at the expense of women and other marginalized groups, but harms men by limiting their emotional range, restricting their relationships with other men, and pressuring them to conform to rigid gender roles.

UNDERSTANDING PATRIARCHY AND ITS PSYCHOANALYTIC FRAMEWORK

We hear it a lot—*patriarchy is bad.* But do we understand what it is? In her book *The Creation of Patriarchy*, Gerda Lerner traces the origins of patriarchal society in Western civilization to the second millennium B.C. and hypothesizes that the rise of patriarchy was not the natural evolution of humanity but rather due to several factors, including the desire for women to take on roles that permitted them to raise their children and the dual development of warfare and agriculture. Since then, women have never enjoyed full freedom—rather experiencing varying degrees of "unfreedom," from slavery to prostitution to forced marriage. Men offered protection and sustenance in return for women's labor. It wasn't always a forced arrangement; women benefited, as did men. However, anyone not paired up in this accepted social model was ostracized and unlikely to enjoy any of the benefits of patriarchy.

Psychoanalytic theory provides a valuable framework for understanding the origins and persistence of patriarchy. From a psychoanalytic perspective, patriarchy is a social system structured around the male psyche. The values, norms, and institutions that sustain patriarchy inherently benefit men and subordinate women. Even when women are revered within their communities and they lead fulfilling and rewarding lives, societies organized in a patriarchal structure ensure most women will remain subjugated or incapable of change.

Fundamental to psychoanalytic theory is the hypothesis that three agencies (developed by Sigmund Freud) form the corpus of a person's personality: the id, the ego, and the superego. The id is the most primitive part of the personality and focuses on satisfying a person's basic needs and desires. The ego is the rational component, the mediator between the id and the superego. The last to fully develop, the superego is the moralistic element of the personality that internalizes social norms and values. The id, the ego, and the superego are in constant conflict with one another, each vying for control. From a psychoanalytic perspective, patriarchy privileges the id over the ego and the superego. In practical terms, patriarchal societies are more likely to value aggression, competition, and dominance over cooperation, compromise, and compassion.

In patriarchal societies, people often have weak superegos—the trait that values compromise, compassion, and a solid moral core—and are more likely to indulge and prioritize destructive behaviors. Men who exhibit stronger superegos are characterized as weak, sensitive, and feminine, since masculinity is frequently associated with aggression. Men with strong superegos tend to be less aggressive, and therefore, judging by patriarchal standards, less masculine. Stripping men of their "masculinity" diminishes them, embarrasses them, and encourages them to suppress their emotions and feelings.

Men often experience restricted emotional bandwidth in patriarchal societies. They learn from their peers, parents, pop culture, and ingrained society structures that to show emotions such as sadness, fear, or vulnerability is inappropriate. Men become isolated and alone and may find it challenging to form close relationships with others. When the few acceptable emotions are rage, anger, and lust, men adapt. *But I know plenty of men who aren't violent toward women*, you think. Or, *My husband has never hit me, so this doesn't apply*. Sensitive, New-Age men also lack full access to their emotions and desires; even men who love women and uphold values like equality for all are adversely affected by patriarchy. So much of how patriarchy impacts identity is subconscious and is so ingrained that many of us don't even recognize patriarchy when we see it. For many men and women, if they're happy, who cares? But happiness isn't indefinite, nor is patriarchy simply about individual relationships. This system disadvantages women and other marginalized groups, so even if men are kind and loving to women, they still benefit from privileges such as, on average, higher wages and greater social agency—and this despite the fact that patriarchy keeps men from expressing their full potential.

Men learn to restrict their relationships with other men to narrowly defined roles, such as those between father and son, brothers, friends, and coworkers. Relationships are often seen as the bedrock of a patriarchal society, but only specific types of relationships. Fathers are expected to be strong and authoritative, while sons are expected to be respectful and obedient. Brotherly relationships fuel loyalty, camaraderie, and competition. Of course, men have friends, but men can't ever feel totally comfortable getting vulnerable with their buddies without being seen as passive and weak—two decidedly negative male attributes in a patriarchal society.

Competition and lack of emotional intimacy are hallmarks of male-male relationships. For many men, this can make it difficult to form supportive friendships and to build a sense of community. Men living under patriarchy may often feel enormous pressure to conform to traditional masculine norms, such as being stoic, aggressive, and competitive. Men may feel pressure to conform to these standards even if they disagree, leading to stress, anxiety, and depression.

Patriarchy harms all men by limiting their acceptable emotional range. Men learn by example and influence (social media, film, literature) that expressing their emotions is not okay, especially those seen as feminine, such as sadness, empathy, or fear. Repressing these emotions can lead men to feel isolated, and then, rather than address their feelings, they will bottle them up, which can hurt their mental and physical well-being.

Even in the 21st century, men, like women, conform to rigid gender roles. These roles often dictate how men dress, behave, and express themselves, thereby limiting the extent to which men can be creative and be their authentic selves.

Patriarchy hinders men from forming close relationships with other men. Men may hesitate to open up to other men about their feelings or problems because they don't want to be seen as weak or unmanly, making it difficult for men to form the kind of supportive relationships that they need. bell hooks argues that patriarchal fathers "cannot love their sons because the rules of patriarchy dictate that they stand in competition with their sons" (hooks, 47). Young men may recall their relationships with their fathers as loving, but with limits, that there was an implicit understanding that father-son bonding will frequently lack true tenderness and love, replaced instead by emptiness and, sometimes, rage (hooks, 49).

Fathers may love their sons and vice versa, but they may lack the ability to forge deep emotional bonds. Men who do not have a positive father figure in their lives may turn to "hypermasculine" heroes as their paternal substitutes. Teenage boys who fail to bond with their fathers may find comfort in musicians, actors, sports stars, and video game characters—even when it's obvious these substitutes will not repair the loss, boys and young men will still grasp at these paternal stand-ins as coping mechanisms for the emotional wounds that never fully heal. These poor stand-ins for true fatherly love and affection warp a young man's identity, leading him to potentially embody a very specific hypermasculinity that may not represent his actual self.

Patriarchy can harm men by limiting their career choices. Good men may be discouraged from pursuing careers traditionally perceived as feminine, even if they are interested in those careers. This may limit their career opportunities and make it more difficult for them to find jobs that they are passionate about.

DISORDERED MASCULINITY IN FILM

Patriarchy doesn't work if it can't offer a robust library of what makes "good" men and "bad" men, and we need look no further than Hollywood for examples. To that end, we began by exploring patriarchal masculinity in *Barbie*, and will also examine historical representation of that social construct in *American Beauty*, the character "Madea" from Tyler Perry's movie franchise, and *Brokeback Mountain* and their depictions of a violent, flawed social system.

American Beauty

American Beauty is a 1999 American black comedy-drama about Lester Burnham, a discontented advertising executive experiencing a midlife crisis when he becomes infatuated with his teenage daughter's best friend, Angela Hayes. Lester's marriage to his wife Carolyn is failing while their insecure daughter, Jane, falls in love with the mysterious new neighbor, Ricky Fitts. The film explicitly explores various themes, including the American Dream, the pursuit of happiness, and the search for meaning in life, but it also serves as a chilling reminder that the patriarchy wins, even if you play by the rules, pulverizing the lives of men and women, who by turns try to conform and flee.

Lester Burnham is trapped in a loveless marriage and a dead-end job. He feels unfulfilled and meaningless until he meets Angela, leading to a newfound zest for life. His obsession with Angela leads him to make "bad" decisions; he rejects patriarchal norms by quitting his job, smoking pot, and working out. Lester's bold rejection of the stereotypical happy nuclear American family is also a rejection of traditional patriarchal values of stoicism, emotional repression, and control. But his death at the hands of Colonel Fitts can be seen as the ultimate consequence for a man who actively rejects patriarchal norms, suggesting bleakly that there is no escape from the patriarchy except through death.

Most of us hear that money brings satisfaction and happiness, and until recently, the common narrative directed toward men was that employment (legal or otherwise) was the surefire way to find that fulfillment. Now, the nature of our work lives is upended—many Americans experience long bouts of unemployment or under-employment—and this destabilized new reality came as a shock for men who have been conditioned to believe that work is an essential pillar to robust self-esteem. As a palliative for those men who no longer find joy or financial benefits from their employment, male egos are provided other ways to feel masculine, such as indulging in online betting, taking illegal drugs, or watching pornography. In "American Beauty," Lester Burnham is burnt out at his dead-end ad agency job and has, for a long time, it appears, been merely going through the motions.[4] He brings home a check, but he is utterly deflated. At the moment of his awakening, Lester realizes that he hates his job and quits (while also threatening blackmail in return for a hefty severance backage) and spends his days flipping burgers with local teens at a burger joint. The rest of his time is spent getting high, working out, and driving around in a new muscle car. Though he says that he feels like he's just waking from being "in a coma for the past twenty years," Lester is still trapped in a patriarchal society. He cannot mend things meaningfully with his wife or authentically share his emotions with her, so he turns to other available diversions. Though Lester embraces the new version of himself, the system is stacked against his success.

Colonel Fitts is a prime example of how patriarchy harms men, even those who attempt to adhere to its strictures mightily. Fitts is deeply insecure about his masculinity and sexuality and overcompensates through physical and psychological violence. This is evident in his relationship with his son, Ricky, whom he belittles and beats, and is implied by the presence of his nearly catatonic wife, Barbara, who does little but sit in the house and shut herself off from the world.

As a closet homosexual, Colonel Fitts is obsessed with sex but is unable to express his sexuality in a healthy way because he has been taught that homosexuality is shameful and true men are stoic and, above all else, straight. The Colonel's deep insecurities and repressions lead him down a path of paranoia; he kills Lester when he suspects his son is having an affair with him. But Fitts indulges in one moment of "weakness" when he kisses Lester, a man who represents everything that Fitts fears and despises and is unable to stand up to because he cannot

---

4. Interesting, isn't it, that Lester works at a place where the goal is to convince people to buy things that will make their lives better, to convince them that their current lives do not meet the patriarchal ideal.

connect or accept his emotions. Lester tells Fitts that he's not gay, causing Fitts to feel overwhelming shame and self-loathing, and to purge
himself of those feelings, he purges the world of Lester. (Lester's murder
is also, coincidentally, the product of an extreme form of unchecked
projective identification.) Would it be fair to say that the Colonel would
not be driven to such extremes were it not for the relentless pressure of
patriarchal demands? Patriarchy teaches men to repress their emotions,
to be ashamed of their sexuality, and to be constantly competing with
other men. In *American Beauty*, the murder of Lester Burnham is the
extreme result of that pressure. The women of the film suffer, too: Fitts's
wife Barbara is a ghost—probably living with the knowledge that her
husband is a closet homosexual—and Lester's wife Carolyn endures all
sorts of misogyny in her own failed bid to break the yokes of patriarchy.

Madea

Over the past two decades, Tyler Perry has written and directed
multi-million-dollar-grossing movies filled with Black actors in leading roles. His megahits star all-Black casts and frequently explore stories with Black women as the leads. His stories explore the themes
of sisterhood, overcoming adversity, love, and power. While Perry's
films are often praised for their representation of Black women, they
have also been criticized for perpetuating patriarchal stereotypes. In
2009, fellow director Spike Lee told participants at the 14th Annual
Black Enterprise Conference that Perry's "imaging is troubling, and it
harkens back to [the racial parody of] Amos n' Andy" (Black Institute,
2009). Other critics argue that his work—especially his portrayal of
Black women—is empowering. Still others, such as Robert J. Patterson,
argue that Perry's success "hinges on his and the audience's inability or
unwillingness to connect to the particularly egregious manifestations
of black patriarchy" (Patterson, 2011, p.9). Perry says that his work

reflects the realities that many Black women face (Lyle, 2011, p. 945). I believe that some of Perry's wildly successful modern-day morality plays reinforce patriarchal masculinity.

In a 2011 issue of *Black Camera, An International Film Journal,* critic Robert J. Patterson analyzes how Perry's films do not directly grapple with patriarchal society but merely identify its worst manifestations, such as sexual abuse and domestic violence, as "representations of black women, family, and gender roles [that] ultimately rearticulate heteronormative patriarchal fantasies" (Patterson, 15).

Perhaps Perry's most well-known recurring character is Madea, Perry's alter-ego inspired by his mother and other strong women of his childhood. Madea is "strong, witty, loving…exactly the PG version of my mother and aunt. She would beat the hell out of you but make sure the ambulance got there in time to make sure they could set your arm back" (NPR, 2012). Much has already been written about Perry and his portrayal of traditional gender roles, especially in relation to women, but I would like to focus here on how Perry's Madea reinforces patriarchal norms and what that means for America's men.

Madea is a ruse—a false promotion of feminism and equality while her agenda aligns with maintaining patriarchal standards. In the 2006 film *Madea's Family Reunion*, the boisterous and no-nonsense matriarch Madea Simmons is tasked with hosting a family reunion. Amidst the chaos of family dynamics, Madea must deal with her rebellious foster daughter, Nikki, while also keeping an eye on her troubled nieces, Lisa and Vanessa.

As the family gathers, tensions rise and old wounds reopen. Lisa is hiding her abusive relationship with her fiancé, Carlos, while Vanessa struggles with her own romantic entanglements and family conflicts.

With her sharp wit and wisdom, Madea tries to guide her family through their struggles, offering tough love, advice, and an overarching message about the importance of family and the power of forgiveness. As the Black "matriarch," Madea looms over everyone in every movie in which she appears. In one scene from *Madea's Family Reunion*, women gather around Madea, who tells them how to fix their lives. Her advice includes standing up for their men. Women are incomplete without a man. Women are responsible for wayward children (including homosexuality), while the men get a free pass to maintain their positions of power and domination. And yet, the men of Perry's fictious universe are static caricatures—yes, they may "set the girls," but they are restricted in their emotional output. Like Ken in *Barbie*, the men of Perry's universe are not allowed to change or evolve much.

As mentioned earlier, in *The Will to Change: Men, Masculinity, and Love*, bell hooks illustrates that contemporary society is patriarchal and discourages men from living to their full potential. She argues that patriarchy is a system of male domination that benefits men at the expense of women and other marginalized groups.

Kenough

Patriarchy harms men through the explicit and implicit use of violence. Men are much more likely than women to be perpetrators and victims of violence. Patriarchy teaches men that violence is acceptable for resolving conflict and expressing emotions. For example, boys learn to "man up" and not to show their feelings, leading to a build-up of anger and resentment, which can erupt into violence. We see this portrayal frequently in American film.

In *Barbie*, Ken's major song, a Matchbox 20 hit from the 1990s has a tendentious refrain. While it may have been the perfect choice for the fragile Kens, parts of it are controversial. "With lyrics like 'I wanna push you around' and 'I wanna take you for granted,' feminist groups at the time condemned the track as misogynistic. Thomas disputed the claims, calling it a 'sad love song' ..." (Wang, 2023)

The '90s was a time of manufactured angst, and nobody wanted to be a victim in a song. So in a weird twist of different times, there's something very problematic about 'Push,' if it wasn't for the innocence of how it was written. But everything about it was about emotional manipulation. It was just about this idea that it's so much easier to find someone you can take advantage of than it is to actually put work into a relationship. (Sumerel, 2023)

While this *may* not have been a way to put women down, the songwriter's explanation sounds open to debate.

Ken has learned that dominating others means throwing one's weight around. In Barbie Land, he has no positive male role models—only Barbie role models. In the real world, he learns that he needs to be pushy and bossy to be taken seriously. It works: Importing Ken's version of the patriarchy overwhelms the Barbies. They have no defenses against it and are effectively brainwashed to please the Kens. Ken's patriarchy focuses on male power and control. Ken and his devotees are thrilled to learn that in the real world, men are superior to women and are therefore in charge and hold more decision-making roles than women. The Kendom replaces Barbie Land.

Clearly, the Kendom is a parody of real-world patriarchy. Ken's society is ridiculous and over the top, but like any good parody, we find elements of truth. The Kendom uses the same principles of male dominance and control that underpin real-world patriarchy.

MALE STUDIES: TO LOVE MEN, TO ALLOW MEN TO LOVE, REQUIRES BREAKING OLD PATTERNS

What emotions are men "allowed" in patriarchy? Anger and lust. In his show "Live at the New York Metropolitan House," Robin Williams joked, "Men. If we can't fuck it, we'll kill it."

Real men get mad. Aggressiveness is proof of a "trad man," as they're called today. Sissies cry—or so the patriarchal trope goes. But deep down, we all want male love—even feminists—and this is a good thing. But to do that we need to recognize patriarchy and identify it as such, in part because it is so ingrained in our social fabric. The 2005 neo-Western drama *Brokeback Mountain* (adapted from the short story by Annie Proulx) is another anti-patriarchal manifesto on par with *American Beauty*.

Ennis Del Mar and Jack Twist forge a profound and forbidden connection in the heart of Wyoming's rugged landscape. Set against the backdrop of the 1960s American West, their paths intertwine during a summer spent herding sheep on the isolated Brokeback Mountain.

Reserved ranch hand Ennis is drawn to the charismatic rodeo cowboy, Jack. One fateful night they share an intimate encounter that ignites a passionate and complex relationship.

Despite their conflicting desires and the societal constraints of the time, Ennis and Jack continue to meet in secret. Their clandestine romance, however, is fraught with challenges and internal struggles, as they grapple with their identities and societal expectations.

As years pass, their lives take diverging paths. Ennis settles into a traditional family life, marrying his fiancée Alma and raising two daughters. Jack pursues his rodeo dreams and marries fellow rodeo rider Lureen in a desperate attempt to conform.

Ennis and Jack cannot sever their profound connection despite their separate lives. They continue to meet in stolen moments. As their lives unfold, they face prejudice, internal conflicts, and the inevitable passage of time. Their love story is a poignant testament to the enduring power of love, even in the face of adversity and social pressures, but beneath it all, patriarchy and its rigid gender roles prevent Ennis and Jack from living their lives the way they want to. Their identities have been carefully crafted for them by a system that does not welcome them as they truly are. The societal norms and expectations associated with masculinity and heterosexuality constrain their ability to express their love openly.

Ennis, deeply entrenched in the traditional values of masculinity, struggles to reconcile his feelings for Jack with the expectations placed upon him, and so suppresses his true self. This internal conflict causes him immense emotional pain and prevents him from fully embracing his identity.

Jack faces the challenges of societal expectations and the fear of rejection from his community. He wrestles with the pressure to conform to the role of a macho cowboy, fearing ostracism and isolation if he were to reveal his true self. This fear leads him to make choices that contradict his true desires, further complicating his life.

Disapproval of same-sex relationships (or, as in this case, bisexuality) during the 1960s adds another layer of complexity to their struggles. The lack of acceptance and understanding of their love makes it difficult for them to find support and validation, further isolating them and preventing them from living authentic lives.

Patriarchy's emphasis on traditional gender roles and societal expectations forces Ennis and Jack to suppress their true selves, leading to a life of secrecy, compromise, and unfulfilled desires. The film highlights how patriarchy can stifle personal growth and a full expression of one's identity.

In the history of American film, male leads are often restricted in the types of relationships they may have with other men; there's the buddy-buddy adventure flick, the rugged cowboys, and the hero and the sidekick. Beyond that, there's been little derivation. Male identity in American film is limited to these few relationships because, as Eve Sedgewick notes in *Between Men*, male-dominated societies only have room for relationship structures that maintain and support patriarchal power.

Matriarchy is not the solution, as it merely replaces one form of oppression with another. Instead, true gender equality, where both men and women are free to express their full range of emotions and pursue their aspirations without societal constraints, is the ideal, but reaching that will require a greater awareness of how patriarchy shapes male identities in ways many men and women don't realize. One of the most powerful forces that drives traditional identity roles is cinema. And, as we see in the films described here, when men are unable to fully realize their true identities, women suffer as well.

REFERENCES

Armengol, J. (December 2007). Gendering men: Re-visions of violence as a test of manhood in American literature. *Atlantis 29.2*, 75–92. ISSN 0210-6124

Bausch, K. (2013). Superflies into superkillers: Black masculinity in film from blaxploitation to new black realism. *The Journal of Pop Culture, 46*(2).

Black Enterprise. (2009). *Spike Lee at the 14th Black Enterprise Conference. Black Enterprise.* Retrieved October 13, 2023, from https://www.youtube.com/watch?v=dK8ibYjciMc.

Fleming, P. J., Gruskin, S., Rojo, F., & Dworkin, S. L. (2015). Men's violence against women and men are inter-related: Recommendations for simultaneous intervention. *Social Science & Medicine (1982), 146*, 249–256. https://doi.org/10.1016/j.socscimed.2015.10.021

Gerwig, G. (2023) *Barbie* [Film]. Warner Bros. Pictures.

Lee, A. (2006). *Brokeback mountain* (Widescreen format) [Film]. Universal Studios Home Entertainment.

hooks, b. (2004). *The will to change: Men, masculinity, and Love*. Washington Square Press.

Mendes, S. (1999). *American beauty* [Film]. DreamWorks Distribution.

NPR. (2012, October 15). Tyler Perry transforms: From Madea to family man. Fresh Air. https://www.npr.org/2012/10/15/162936803/tyler-perry-transforms-from-madea-to-family-man

Patterson, R. J. (2011). "'Woman thou art bound'": Critical spectatorship, black masculine gazes, and gender problems in Tyler Perry's movies. *Black Camera, 3*(1), 9. https://doi.org/10.2979/blackcamera.3.1.9

Perry, T. (2005). *Madea's family reunion* (Standard format) [Film]. Lions Gate Home Entertainment.

Sedgewick, E. (1985). *Between men: English literature and male homosocial desire*. Columbia University Press.

Sumerel, A. (2023). The Use of Matchbox Twenty's 'Push' in 'Barbie' is Brilliant, and Not Just Because of Ryan Gosling's Epic Performance. Retrieved from, https://eulaliemagazine.com/2023/09/matchbox-twenty-push-barbie-brilliant-not-just-because-of-ryan-gosling-performance/

Wang, J. (2023). How Greta Gerwig landed that memorable '90s song for the Kens in Barbie. Retrieved from https://ew.com/movies/ryan-gosling-self-conscious-matchbox-twenty-ken-song-barbie/

Essay Three

Barbie on the Couch

*How Therapy Might Have Changed Her World and Ours;
A Snippet of Her Analysis*

> *It is literally impossible to be a woman. You are so beautiful,
> and so smart, and it kills me that you don't think you're
> good enough. Like, we have to always be extraordinary, but
> somehow we're always doing it wrong....I'm just so tired of
> watching myself and every single other woman tie herself into
> knots so that people will like us. And if all of that is also true
> for a doll just representing women, then I don't even know.*
> —BARBIE, the movie (2023)

In the *Barbie* movie, Average American mom Gloria delivers this exasperated and poignant monologue lamenting the impossible standards imposed on women. In an interview with the *Atlantic*, filmmaker Greta Gerwig noted that she and everyone on set—even the men—cried during the filming of this scene, "because they [men] have their own speech they feel they can't ever give." And at the end of this scene, nobody's there to provide answers, because there aren't any; yes, women (and, by extension, Barbie) are held to unrealistic standards, but beyond acknowledging them, is there anything we can do to fix it?

Fixing the world and how women are expected to behave in it may be an impossible task, but women can get help as they navigate it. But what about Barbie? Sure, she's a plastic plaything, but, just as we are willing to accept the *Barbie* movie plot, I wondered what it might have been like if Barbie had been a patient in psychoanalysis. Barbie has served as inspiration and object of fantasy since her creation. Imagine if she knew about these projections—how would that impact her psyche? Surely, she'd need therapy. Below is an imagined scenario of what we both might have learned from this type of internal journey.[5]

FIRST PHONE CONTACT

Barbie emailed me when she was 37 years old and recently transplanted to Washington, DC, from California. She received my name from a mutual acquaintance and asked if I had time to see her for a consultation. I agreed and set up an initial exploratory meeting to discuss her needs and to see if we might be a good patient-analyst fit.

OUR FIRST MEETING

Barbie appeared anxious when she arrived in my office, fidgeting with her hair and biting her nails. She said she had never talked about her problems to anyone because the world thought she was perfect, and she felt bound to uphold that image. Lately, however, she said she thought she was going to "lose it" because of all the pressure she was experiencing.

"From the first day of my life that I can remember, I felt like I wanted to fall in love, get married, have children, and live like a real person, but I can't," Barbie began. "People have flaws, but that's not my destiny. I'm Barbie, I must be perfect."

---

5. See Essay One for Barbie's full origin story.

"What has that felt like for you?" I asked. A tear rolled down her porcelain skin. After pausing for a couple of minutes, she responded.

"I hate it. I can't ever make a mistake. Everyone talks about my looks—my perfect body and my beautiful hair and my exquisite breasts, and my lipstick and makeup, the list goes on and on."

"You must feel like you have the weight of the world on your shoulders," I commented. Barbie burst into tears. She cried for several minutes until she finally said, "Yes, that's exactly how I feel. Little girls and teens believe they can become like their favorite Barbie, but who am I? I'm a hollow plastic doll. If I were a real person, I'd have no sense of who I am because I was created to please other people. I was literally made of plastic—God, what an awful thing that is for the environment, all that toxic waste." She paused briefly to wipe away her tears before continuing.

"In the 1950s, women *knew* their place was in the home. From what I've read, people seemed to understand their roles in life. Women were oppressed, but at least there seemed to be clarity and they weren't expected to be everything to everyone. When women started to rebel in the late 1960s and '70s and speak up for themselves, I was left behind. I had to remain perfect. As a sort of consolation, Mattel dreamed up all sorts of jobs and positions for me, but they were in name only. No one *actually expected* me to represent a president or a judge. Whether I was President Barbie or Flower Power Barbie, I was nothing more than a model for new clothes and accessories. I was never supposed to feel especially empowered, and I don't think the girls who played with me felt empowered, either."[6]

Barbie continued to talk about how she wanted to rebel but felt trapped. Our time soon came to an end that day.

---

6. Certainly, our Barbie can't know with total certainty whether the girls who played with her likeness were overwhelmed or inspired by her. We do have studies that reveal greater self-dissatisfaction among girls who play with Barbie dolls versus girls who don't, but we also have anecdotal evidence where girls who played with Barbie grew up to become creative professionals and exhibited normal and robust self-confidence. (Consider, for example, Gloria in the Barbie movie—she adored playing with Barbie and seems more or less normal. She does experience a depression. See: illustrating "Irrepressible Thoughts of Death Barbie," but she does not attribute those feelings to Barbie.)

"Do you think you can help me?" she asked as she looked at the clock. "I want to do this right, and I'm not getting any younger. I want to be analyzed. I like the way you listen and let me talk. That's not something I've encountered very often. I know I'm all mixed up, don't know myself, and I don't have much information about my background. but I want to find out who I am for my sake and for girls around the world so they can understand that I am *not* the answer to their struggles. I'm not who they think I am. A lot of people don't take firm stands on much of anything. They don't know who they are, either. Some people are so inflexible it makes it hard to speak with them because they only care about themselves. Maybe if the word got out that Barbie finally knew who she was, it could make a difference."

As I listened to Barbie's struggle to know herself, I knew I wanted to help her figure out her queries about her internal and external world. Would she be a candidate for psychoanalysis, or would psychotherapy be more appropriate?

Eventually, we set up three more appointments and assessment for psychoanalysis.

BARBIE BECOMES REAL FOR THE SAKE OF HER TREATMENT

I learned a lot during my initial meetings with Barbie. In preparation, I reviewed a couple of recent publications on the benefits of analysis as well as my own writing on the topic.[7] In 2019, I coined a term that I believe captures the essence of how and why people change, called Redactional Identification. This process involves change within the self

---

7. Kevin and Vamik Volkan wrote a book reminding practitioners that psychoanalytic psychotherapy can help patients deal with emotional problems. Psychoanalysis is a deeper treatment that "leads to making positive structural modifications in the analysand's mind and mental functions. However, going through a long-term psychoanalytic psychotherapy may also help patients to develop more adaptive and less anxiety-provoking ways to live."

that comes into being in concert with another person, a safe person who allows something different to develop.

As this new way of navigating in the world allows for unconscious thoughts to enter one's conscious mind since psychological safety is more present, a new way of being develops. At the same time, with the help of the other person, a way of living with intention emerges.[8]

Equipped with this knowledge, I decided to start Barbie's treatment four times a week on the couch, not only because she wanted an analysis but because I thought she had sufficient ego strengths and other characteristics that would allow her to withstand the regression inherent in an analysis. Regression in psychoanalysis means there is an unconscious defense that leads one to return to an earlier way of being. She seemed to have the capacity for self-exploration while realizing that current behavior is related to our past experiences. She also seemed to feel an appropriate level of guilt and seemed to be able to take responsibility for her life, this despite knowing that a portion of her adolescence and the years that followed were dominated by the wishes of others.

Barbie was clearly depressed and anxious as she dealt with the knowledge that she existed to please others above all else, that she was merely a plastic pleasure or hatred vessel. Barbie knew she wanted a different kind of life with an intimate partner she loved since she never loved Ken. She was vaguely familiar with the concept of the unconscious parts of our minds from reading she had done. She had a burning desire to get on with the rest of her life without being controlled by

---

8. The new experience with a safe person allows for the development of something different. As a new state of mind emerges, it eventually becomes a conscious process that includes intention. A new element comes into play as the need for unconscious protection yields to awareness within the self-structure. This process helps to solidify change. It is a conscious part of one's being that involves more than eradicating deplorable elements of one's being or tolerating one's own aggression. More than "getting rid of" or "putting up with" or "coming to endure" an unwanted part of the self, this new intentional process involves awareness of creating a new version of an old story. I am calling this newly developed, conscious process redactional identification, i.e., a way of creating a desirable aspect of oneself, learned at least in part from another person, perhaps directed by Alford's (2016) benevolent "inner other." This "inner other" is an active, knowable, and creative part of one's inner being.

Mattel executives. If she was going to remain to be Barbie, at least she wanted to make decisions for herself.

I decided Barbie would be a good candidate for analysis. While this is not the only criteria, knowledge of a person's early years with his or her parents helps an analyst determine whether or not to recommend analysis as a treatment of choice. For those with very traumatic backgrounds, another treatment modality might be suggested. Since I had little to no information about Barbie's real parents, her early history was not something I could count on to help determine whether psychoanalysis was the best treatment for her. What I did know was that I liked her and felt immediately connected to her, something else that one often considers when thinking about optimal options for therapy.

Barbie's curiosity about her life, including her inner world, was another promising sign that she was ready for analysis, but she did seem to be overly willing to please others. While I realized this could present a problem if she were not able to express her negative and aggressive feelings toward me as well as others, she showed spunk, so I felt confident that she would eventually be able to express herself when she was disappointed or angry.[9]

When I told Barbie I was recommending analysis, she cried for

---

9. The characteristics that make a patient desirable or undesirable to work with are not very different from those involved in choosing lovers, friends, or colleagues. Those who are stable, dependable, reliable, achievement oriented, inquisitive, sensitive, concerned, and attractive are more generally sought after than their opposites. They are also likely to succeed in their work, in personal relationships, and as patients in analysis. Further, it is likely that a largely favorable and facilitating early environment provided the beginnings of this pattern of relatively satisfying encounters with the world. In contrast, the unacceptable analytic patient is often expert in finding ways to fail and to elicit withdrawal in others. It is likely that friends and colleagues are prone to retreat in much the same way as prospective analysts. The patient's early life is probably fraught with subtle or obvious parental insensitivities, and the child grows up either treating others in that same manner and/or expecting others to do as the parents did. The more severely disturbed and less desirable patients are prone to act out and terminate or miss sessions, withdraw and produce boredom, and/or make excessive demands and attempts at intrusion into the analyst's personal life. They will not be primarily cooperative, they strike fear into the analyst via suicide threats or attempts, or they embarrass the analyst by possibly requiring hospitalization or by becoming publicly bizarre. Ultimately, and perhaps most significantly, they are less likely to reach analytic goals and thereby are less likely to provide the analyst with some feeling of one's work bearing fruit (Hirsch, 1984).

most of the session. "Finally! Someone is listening to me," she said between sobs. "Going way back, I never wanted the Handlers to make me into Barbie. I was happier in Germany as Bild Lilli. I had a *personality*. People knew who I was, and I did too. I was a spicy, sassy young woman who men loved.

"I think some girls in high school liked me too. Some were jealous, but I was friendly to everyone and was game for most things. I think that's why they weren't too bothered by how I looked. I was pretty but nice. Don't get me wrong, I had plenty of disappointments when my grades weren't good or when my strict parents got mad at me, but all things considered, I think my teen years were okay. Then the Handlers showed up and stole me from my country." Barbie began sobbing. "It was like a kidnapping that no one knew about or as if I was a sex-trafficked case." Barbie paused and then took something from her purse. She asked, "Can I read you what they wrote about me in this book by Tanya Lee Stone, *The Good, The Bad, and The Barbie: A Doll's History and her impact on Us?*"

To that I said, "It seems like it's hard for you to tell me your story. I think reading may be less painful." Barbie was silent for several minutes and said, "It's so painful to remember the past, about the person the Handlers stole. If I can read parts of my life, it's like hearing about someone else. It makes this process easier for me." Realizing this was a defensive maneuver she might have needed to feel like she could keep herself on track, I said, "You can read the story about your like if you'd like. However, experiencing the feelings that go with the words is also important."

Barbie considered this for a moment. "I will tell you and I will let myself feel what things were really like. Today, I think I will read some too." I took this as a positive sign that she didn't feel she needed to comply with my thoughts about reading versus telling me about her life, so I didn't comment further. After a minute or two, she took out the book and began reading. Here's a portion of what she read:

Why does she irritate, even enrage, so many people and attract so many others to leap to her defense? She is just a doll, after all. But she is not just a doll. Yes, Mattel made her an icon, but not without help. It started at the moment of her inception. That very first television commercial, with Barbie as an active companion, planted the illusion in our minds that she was "real." The idea was so powerful, it stuck.

"That's so unfair!" Barbie shouted as she took a break from reading. "How can I be both a representation of a woman and blamed for women's issues when I'm also just a piece of plastic? I'm going to keep reading. Look, here's my 'origin story!'"

Mattel reinforced the desire in us to make Barbie real by creating an entire life story for her. A series of novels published in the 1960s established who she was, complete with birth date, parents, and a significant other, Ken. According to the novels, Barbara (aka Barbie) Millicent Roberts grew up in Willows, Wisconsin, where she lived with her parents, George and Margaret Roberts.... The novels establish Barbie as a modern, independent kind of girl who was not going to be bound by the 1950s stereotypes she felt kept her mother tied to the house.... We have bought into the idea of Barbie being a "real" doll and helped make her the icon—and subject of controversy—that she is (Stone, 2010).

Barbie paused and then said, "That's the part I can't stand the most. Talking about a false version of me. I'm not Barbie, I'm Lilli." She then started sobbing again. I reached over and handed her a box of tissues. "Thank you," she said as she grabbed a bunch. "This is one of the kindest things anyone has ever done for me."

I was a bit perplexed. It was a simple gesture to give a crying woman a tissue. Why would that have moved her so much? She continued to cry as she blotted her face with half the box of tissues. After ten minutes, she calmed down.

"You must think I'm a nut for thanking you for tissues, but it wasn't the tissues that tapped into all those tears. It was the recognition that someone understood what I needed versus what was good for them."

"It sounds like life was tough for you when you left Germany and moved to the Handlers' place," I responded. The tears started again but only briefly this time.

"I wouldn't say the Handlers were mean, they were just selfish. They used me for their own gain and never thought about my earlier life. It's as if they deprogrammed me to be someone else other than Lilli—that was my given name." As she left that day, she thanked me for listening to her story.

As the initial phase of treatment continued, Barbie talked a lot about her constant work schedule at Mattel as a model and an administrative assistant. She seemed to work day and night. She also spent a good deal of time telling me what a great therapist I was, to which I usually said it seemed like having a very good analyst was important to her. She always agreed and said things like "You are the best therapist in the world. You are my lifeline to reality. You've saved me from a phony, plastic world of fake people and meaningless banter that occurs all the time at fancy parties."

While I knew Barbie was idealizing me, it seemed like something she needed to do to survive her jet-set life with the Handlers. This phase of our work together lasted for a couple of years. During those early sessions, she frequently turned her head while lying on the couch to look at me. I thought at the time that she wanted to see if my eyes were opened. One day, I shared that idea with her. Barbie didn't say anything, and when the session ended, she gathered her coat and left in silence.

I was surprised at this type of exit because it was the first time she left without saying good-bye, but I thought it might have signaled a shift in our work. I suspected her idealization of me might have ended, which I thought might have heralded in the middle phase of treatment.

When Barbie arrived for her next session, she went to the couch and was silent for approximately ten minutes. She appeared to be angry.

"I think I've figured out why you are so nice to me and don't point out my Lilli-type flaws like the Handlers did and still do," she began. "You want to make me into a robotic person just like they did. But you have a different style. They formed me into their own image. Now you know who I am or could become, but you don't give me suggestions or tell me what to do. You don't tell me who I should date, how I can get a different job, what I can do to have some fun, or anything else. You're just nice to me, which is better than nothing." Barbie paused briefly, then asked herself out loud, "What am I doing? I'm railing on you, but why?"

"You're angry because I seem just like the people who took you from your homeland and now aren't giving you what you need," I said. Barbie nodded.

"I know in my head this isn't right, but you feel like them. They stripped me of my identity without knowing what they were doing. You, on the other hand, you know what you are doing, you know what I need but you won't tell me."

Before I could respond, she continued.

"There's another thing that's been gnawing away at me, but I can't put my finger on it."

"It seems like I am withholding things from you, as if I could help you if I told you things to do. In the absence of me telling you how to live your life, you are forgetting something that might be important," I offered.

Barbie smirked. "I'll give you one thing, you've got that right. I do think you could guide me, give me advice. Your patients must tell you how they meet people, but you don't share that. You are just as bad as the Handlers—they stuff me with what I don't need, and you withhold what you know would help me, yet you won't give it to me. I have too much and too little." With that comment our time ended, and she left.

The analysis proceeded in much the same way over the next three years as her anger and guilt toward the Handlers manifested in various outbursts.

This dynamic continued until she came in one day with a smile on her face.

"I think I have an inkling of what's been happening. I think I've figured out your strategy."

I asked her to elaborate.

"I had a dream that I was on an old shipwreck that ran aground in shallow waters close to an island. The wreck happened during a horrific storm. It was like an old pirate ship you see in movies. I thought I was lost forever." Barbie paused before continuing.

"I was treated like a slave. No one abused me, but I worked sixteen hours a day gathering food for the people who had survived, cleaning nonstop since the captain was a clean freak. I also had to cook with other people who lived in steerage, people who were all escaping something. I didn't think I was going to die, but life was pretty bad."

I waited as Barbie drew breath and smiled as she launched into the next part of her dream narrative.

"Then the dream shifted, and I was in an office where I was surfing the net. I saw your glass-blowing website. Then I woke up." I asked her what came to her mind about the dream.

"I never told you this, but when my friend in California recommended you, I looked you up. I saw your therapy website and then I found another one. I looked it up again this morning. Now I get what you are trying to do." Barbie then pulled a piece of paper from her pocket and read to me what she had copied from my glass-blowing website.

"'I've now encountered another mode of exploration and self-expression, glass sculpture. This new way of illustrating my perspective on life came about by learning how to blow glass and work with metal. In this quite different world, images from my childhood come to life as abstract objects from the sea....I view it as a dance between two people, a tango of sorts wherein pieces evolve as the artist and assistant work with each unique gather. New possibilities for forms arise as the dancers respect and control the properties of hot glass. At times a piece must fall; at others it must be lifted, while always requiring it to be turned. It is this interplay between two artists that creates a unique structure, one that cannot be replicated. Much like my work with patients wherein two people create interpretations and come to understand the unique meaning of an individual's life, glassblowing and metal pieces evolve as representations of one's life with the help of another.'"

Barbie neatly folded the paper and looked directly at me. "You're trying to help me help myself," she said, smiling broadly. "Instead of telling me *what* to do, you are trying to help me figure out who I am in life and who I want to become."

THE BEGINNING OF THE END

After that session, Barbie began to work hard in therapy to try to understand what she wanted in life and why. Now, after years of working together, Barbie stopped resisting my interpretations. It felt like our work became more of a collaboration. She said she was becoming more like Lilli, who knew what she wanted and went after it. Although she didn't want to taunt men as she did when she was a teen, she did want to find a partner with whom she could share her life. She also knew she didn't want to be at the beck and call of the Handlers, who by this time had their hands full with legal issues involving tax evasion. Instead of being everyone's Barbie doll, she wanted to do something good for the world. She also wanted to know about fake news and the proliferation of false information.[10]

Barbie was fascinated by "Pizzagate," the conspiracy theory that Hillary Clinton and fellow Democrats were luring children to the basement of a DC pizzeria as part of a pedophilic, blood-drinking sex ring that helped propel Trump to the presidency in 2016.

Barbie was shocked by this story—that such patently false and spaceshot conspiracy theories not only existed but thrived in contemporary America. She decided to end her career at Mattel and looked for a position on Capitol Hill so she could learn about how our democracy works and how she could help bring positive change to our country.

Thanks to her fame, she initially got a job as a legislative assistant and worked for a well-respected senator for several years, where she learned about the impact climate change was having on our environment and how the internet was used to spread erroneous information. Eventually, she went back to school and got a degree in environmental law and became deeply committed to environmental policy. Her experience eventually led her to help American corporations collaborate with other companies on cleaning up the environment. While completing her graduate degree, she met a man who was a couple of years older and became engaged two years after finishing her academic work.

In the spring of 2011, Barbie was with a man with whom she shared many things in her personal life and in her work. Since she finally discovered who she was as a person, her true identify as a woman and as a partner in an intimate relationship emerged. She also became a spokesperson for climate change, which included the right to learn about and then become someone who could say what was on her mind without fear of reprisal.

---

10. Fake news and false information have proliferated since at least the Roman Empire when Octavian launched a smear campaign against Mark Antony (Posetti & Mathews, 2018).

THE LAST PHASE OF HER ANALYSIS

Of the many ways the termination phase plays out in analysis, some amount of regression to old patterns of thinking is expected. But this regression is generally minor when weighed against a patient's consolidation of gains. Mourning is also a part of the process, which was the case in Barbie's treatment, since a great deal of this period involved mourning the losses of what she missed in life and could never have again. She could never be the carefree adolescent that Lilli was so many years ago. Her spirited nature had been taken away, first by the Handlers and then reinforced by her own sense of inferiority because she hadn't had the opportunity to develop her own sense of industry (or agency) (known in psychoanalysis as Erikson's fourth state of development). Failure at this stage led to her lack of awareness about what she could achieve in life as well as her inability to learn who she was as a person. This also thwarted her ability to continue to form her own identity as Lilli once the Handlers stole her sense of self and replaced it with their own needs.

Barbie also felt guilty for a long time about the way she treated Ken. Although she came to realize that she never really liked him romantically, she thought she might have led him on. Eventually, she concluded that since she didn't know who she was as a person, she couldn't know who she was as a member of a couple.

Originally, this was only a *thought*, but she still *felt* guilty. However, in time she realized she wasn't responsible for the Handlers' creation of a boyfriend she really didn't know. We also talked about the possibility that Mattel might have created this fantasy. Had they projected this image of Barbie as the star and Ken as a wannabe boyfriend in a relationship that never materialized for their own gain? While that interpretation seemed plausible to Barbie, she thought it was only the first part of a more sinister side of Mattel's characteristically self-promoting way of operating.

She thought it was possible that they weren't ever interested in Ken being a big star since there was no real money in a Ken doll. Barbie was the moneymaker. She came to believe they didn't want girls or boys to suddenly crave all kinds of Kens at the expense of losing interest in Barbie. Barbie was the star who made Mattel money, so whatever happened to Ken wasn't important. He was replaceable. She also came to believe that Mattel projected their blasé attitude about Ken onto her, which led her to believe he wasn't important. She could treat Ken in a dismissive way because he wasn't important to Mattel.

She also thought another story could have helped people more if they had a loving relationship, one which showcased feelings of respect and equality felt by men toward women. One day during this final phase in her analysis, she talked about Ken.

"Imagine if Ken had been outspoken about the problems in our society with domestic violence and organized protests that encouraged men to treat woman with dignity? What a different world this might be."

While this was her stance at times, at other times she would go back to criticizing herself for how she had instigated the poor treatment of Ken, saying things like "I intensely dislike myself for blaming anyone else for Ken's situation. I used him, made fun of him, and treated him like he was a nobody. It wasn't the Handlers' fault, at least not entirely. I resented them for years, but why? I wasn't held hostage. I just never found my own voice. I was averse to conflict, didn't rebel, and always did what they wanted me to do." Although she thought she knew what was right for her, she often pretended to be superficial when she had ideas of her own.

After being angry with the Handlers, Mattel, and then with me in the transference, she came to realize she was also annoyed with herself. In this final stage of our work together, she took some responsibility for her behavior. While she had been burdened by a harsh superego severely criticizing herself for what others had done in the middle phase of our work, later she developed a more benign superego.

"I've been angry at the Handlers for so many years, but why? What am I really angry about? Despite all my issues with them, they gave me a good life. I was the most popular doll in the world. I think my new outlook has something to do with my sense of disappointment in myself. That's why I was so upset in the movie when my feet started to become flat. I guess I was depressed but faked it for so many years."

To this I said, "For a good deal of your life, you have turned your anger about the world on yourself."

"That's hard to hear, but I can't really deny that's how I've experienced much of my life, whether it was conscious or not," Barbie said. "But what would happen if I accepted and forgave the Handlers and myself? What if I turned the aggression toward something else that really matters in life, like global warming? If I could use that energy toward something that really matters to me, now that I am more at peace with the way my life turned out, it wouldn't be just Ruth or Ken or you, or even myself that held my aggression for me." She paused for several minutes then added, "Wouldn't it be more powerful if I could direct my energy toward things that could make the world a better place? I could become a spokesperson for cleaner air or start movements to clean up our polluted oceans."

After that session, Barbie again recalled what she remembered from my artist statement, that we must "work together to form something new," that two people can "create interpretations and come to understand the unique meaning of an individual's life."

"I would literally need your help forever, but you will always be part of who I've become as a person in my own right because you helped me figure out who I am in life," she said. "For one thing, I've become a woman with a voice who has something to say, in particular, about our environment."

In the last year of her analysis, Barbie got married and had a daughter at the age of 42. She named the baby Lilli, because she said Lilli was real as a person and Barbie was not.

Although she initially sent me cards now and then about new developments in her life, I most often heard about her from what was reported in the news.

Barbie became a journalist for a national newspaper and then a spokesperson for environmental changes that she initiated through dialogues with various countries. She was well known for her position on our need to repair the damage we have caused by polluting our planet. Since our last session she learned a lot about AI and how it is helpful in so many areas of our lives. She talked a lot about the importance of making grids more efficient which can increase renewable sources of energy while reducing the planet's carbon footprint.

Her stance on what she believed was possible often appeared in her speeches, "We have the technology, now all we need to do is to learn to talk with each other about the best ways to collaborate so we can solve the problems we have created in productive ways in order to save our planet."

After not hearing from Barbie for quite a while she sent an email to me when she found a book review I wrote which was mentioned in Essay One. From what she conveyed in her message, Barbie was pleased to know that people were challenging themselves to consider future uses of technology. She indicated that she appreciated knowing about the new thinking that was emerging that involved our changing world. She quoted the authors cited below. "Technology not only changes the way people live and experience the world and each other; it changes who and what they are and what it means to be human" (Knafo, D. & Lo Bosco, R., 2017).

My observations about this book were something she also seemed to like.

This thought-provoking book poses many questions about the future while expanding on the meaning of perversion by defining it as much more than abnormal or deviant sexual behavior.

These authors boldly predict how travelers on the 'crooked path' flout societal norms as they change the landscape of human behavior. The phenomenon of attaching ourselves to smartphones and computers while counting on social media "friends" to replace our need for real human connections is raising questions about the distinction between aberrance and mere personal preference. (Messina, 2020, para. 3)

She added that in Knafo's recent work that connects catfishing—a word that means camouflaging your real identity on the internet—with Donald Winnicott's ideas about transitional objects which was a very useful way of combining psychoanalysis with new technology.

As she described it in her email, it seems as though Knafo is suggesting that posing as an anonymous person to connect with someone online might be a bit like the way infants use their primary object (Winnicott was talking about a young child's mother or primary caregiver). She added a quote from the article because she knew of my interest in the topic.

A final Winnicott (Citation1971) notion that applies to catfishing is the use of the object. Winnicott (Citation1971) proposed a developmental sequence that progresses from object relating, during which the object is part self and part other, to use of the object, which is achieved when one recognizes the object's own independence and autonomy. Using the object involves the object having a separate existence that is "real in the sense of being part of shared reality, not a bundle of projections" (p. 88). Catfish are stuck in Winnicott's object relating phase (Knafo, 2021).

Barbie also said that she was pleased to learn about the connection between AI and fundamental aspects of psychoanalytic thinking after reading, *Algorithmic unconscious: why psychoanalysis helps in understanding AI* by Luca M. Possati. She seemed particularly fascinated by what the author said about identity and identification since these concepts had been such an important part of her life, "I argue that AI is a new stage in the human identification process, namely, a new development of the unconscious identification. After the imaginary and symbolic registers, AI is the third register of identification" (Possati, 2020).

That AI could be useful is recognizing mental illnesses was also something that seemed significant to Barbie because AI could detect schizophrenia from illogical sentence structures while sudden shifts in tone and mood could identify depression and bipolar disorders.

REFERENCES

Cozolino, L. J. (2010). In *The Neuroscience of Psychotherapy: Healing the Social Brain*. New York, W.W. Norton & Co.

Dewan, A. (2024). Scientists say they can use AI to solve a key problem in the quest for near-limitless clean energy. Retrieved February 24, 2024, from https://www.cnn.com/2024/02/21/climate/nuclear-fusion-ai-climate-solution/index.html.

Hirsch, I. (1984). Toward a more subjective view of analyzability. *American Journal of Psychoanalysis 44*, 169–182

Messina, K. (2019). *Misogyny, projective identification and mentalization*. London, Routledge.

Messina, K. (2021). *Aftermath: Healing from the Trump presidency*. PI Press.

Posetti, J., & Matthews, A. (2018). *A short guide to the history of "fake news" and disinformation*. International Center for Journalists. https://www.icfj.org/sites/default/files/2018-07/A%20Short%20Guide%20to%20History%20of%20Fake%20News%20and%20Disinformation_ICFJ%20Final.pdf

Possati, L. (2020). Algorithmic unconscious: why psychoanalysis helps in understanding AI. Palgrave Commun 6, 70 https://doi.org/10.1057/s41599-020-0445-0

Stone, T. (2010). *The good, the bad and The Barbie: A doll's history and her impact on us*. Viking.

Volkan, K., & Volkan, V. (2023). *How the mind works: Concepts and cases in psychoanalysis and psychotherapy* (pp. 3–6). Phoenix Publishing House. Kindle Edition.

Winnicott, D. W. (1971). *Playing and reality*. Penguin.

Essay Four

Barbie's Various Roles

*Social Media Change Agent, Environmentalist,
and AI Specialist*

*One of the penalties of an ecological education
is to live alone in a world of wounds.*
—ALDO LEOPOLD, *A Sand County Almanac:
And Sketches Here and There* (1949)

Conservationist and author Aldo Leopold was one of the earliest observers to codify the phenomenon of grief associated with the disappearance of plants, animals, and ecosystems. Today, humans across the globe confront losses in the natural world that have significantly altered their way of life, and these changes have mental health consequences as well. It's time to recognize, if not embrace, our collective grief for our imperiled planet, and mobilize our efforts to mitigate the damage before it's too late.

Whether Barbie herself can directly save the environment is debatable, but she can be a force for good by raising awareness and inspiring action. This essay continues with the hypothetical assumption that Barbie is real, has completed psychoanalysis, and is ready to take on the environmental crisis.

As imagined in Essay Three, Barbie completes analysis and becomes a journalist and a spokesperson for environmental change. Barbie believes that humans have the technology to prevent the worst of climate change; now we humans need to collaborate to save the planet. We can only do that through active listening and mutual respect. Barbie has learned that you can only force people to do things for a little while. Eventually, they revolt. To save the planet, everyone has a voice that deserves to be heard, and disagreement should be encouraged. That means the paper logging executives and oil company CEOs are just as important in helping solve this crisis as are the grassroots environmentalists. Here is what she learns.

Barbie was not pleased to realize that her very existence contributed to massive overconsumption and the world's pollution. According to Mattel, 58 million Barbies are sold every year—that's 100 every minute worldwide (Schmidt, 2020). Many of those dolls eventually end up in landfills: Each weighs 182 grams of plastic. Each doll's production, creation, and transport produces 660 grams of carbon emissions, producing roughly 10.9 billion grams of plastic and 40 billion grams of carbon emissions annually (Ruffin, 2024). And this is just for Barbie dolls.

Further, Barbie contains six types of plastic, from ethylene-vinyl acetate for her arms to polypropylene and PVC for her legs. This combination of plastic makes Barbie challenging to recycle. And 80% of all toys (90% of which are constructed of plastic) wind up in landfills barely six months after purchase; this churn is unsustainable (Kapfunde, 2019).

Change seems to be underway: Mattel announced an initiative to create a circular manufacturing system by 2030 with 100% recycled, recyclable, or "bio-based plastic" for its products (Mattel, 2024). Customers can also return their old Barbies and other toys to Mattel as part of the company's "Playback" initiative that repurposes the plastic into different products. In 2022, the company launched "Barbie Loves the Ocean," made from plastic trash collected in Baja, Mexico (Woody, 2022). And there is Renewable Energy Engineer Barbie, who debuted in 2022 in a 100% recycled cardboard box and whose outfit is certified Carbon Neutral (Lange, 2023).

None of this completely solves the consumption crisis, and the energy required to repurpose these toys hasn't been reported, meaning it's likely to be quite carbon intensive. However, it is a start. Another good step would be to simply buy less: Parents buy their children an estimated 40 pounds of toys annually—again, most of that headed straight for the dump.

HOW PROJECTIVE IDENTIFICATION AND CLIMATE CHANGE DENIALISM HAVE EXACERBATED THE PROBLEM.

Climate change denialism has flourished in recent years, much of that due to the underlying psychological phenomenon of projective identification. In the United States, Donald Trump has given more credence to climate change denialism than any other single person in recent memory.

While it's true that Trump is not personally responsible for climate change—and he did not set our situation in motion—his administration's policies and proclamations set climate mitigation efforts back years. In 2020, *The New York Times* reported that one of Trump's most profound legacies would be climate change. (This was written before the January 6 insurrection on the Capitol, but I think these are Trump's top two legacies.) Trump's climate rollbacks occurred at a time when the global level of greenhouse gases entered a higher concentration in the atmosphere, meaning that some of the larger weather events we're seeing now, like mega-storms, rising sea levels, and intense heatwaves, are irreversible (Davenport, 2020).

Trump sent mixed messages during the early days of his presidency: His acknowledgment that climate change is not a "hoax" stood in stark contrast to his memorable refusal to believe the 2017 National Climate Assessment produced by US government scientists. The announced withdrawal from the Paris Agreement only months after it had gone into effect under the Obama Administration (Trump, 2019), along with unprecedented rollbacks of significant climate and environmental policies (Popovich, 2020), did not instill much hope in those Americans who recognized the need to address climate change to avoid further global catastrophe.

A statement released in 2020 by a group of nine leading agencies decried the Trumpian attack on the environment:

> Donald Trump's administration has unleashed an unprecedented assault on our environment and the health of our communities. His policies threaten our climate, air, water, public lands, wildlife, and oceans; no amount of his greenwashing can change the simple fact: Donald Trump has been the worst President for our environment in history. Unfortunately, our children will pay the costs of this President's recklessness. Our organizations have repeatedly fought back against these attacks, and we will continue to fight to ensure that our kids don't bear the brunt of the Trump administration's anti-environmental agenda (LaRue, 2020).

While a growing chorus of neuroscientists, psychologists, psychiatrists, and researchers in many other fields of study echo the urgent need to interact with our outdoor environment to be mentally healthy, what we need to do that—have clean, breathable air—is becoming less available. According to Martin Hayden, vice president of policy and legislation at Earthjustice, Trump assaulted the "basic safeguards" to protect or clean up our water and air. He calls out multiple parties, including "[c]oal and oil lobbyists installed at the highest levels of government tasked with eviscerating our bedrock environmental laws" and "[s]ecretive schemes to ensure that the public never gets a chance to hear about or speak out against any of it" (LaRue, 2020). Hayden added, "The only power that's restrained these corporate cronies in office is the power of the law."

Now, in 2024, Trump is running for reelection, and frankly, the climate cannot handle another Trump presidency. He called it a hoax and denied its existence the first time around; you can bet he will only redouble his efforts to forget about it with another term in office. And if America doesn't do anything about climate change, you can be sure many other countries will feel disinclined to do anything about it (Schlanger, 2023).

To make progress, we need a sustained paradigm shift that involves changing how we pollute our planet. Only by engaging in an open dialogue about global warming—and facing what Al Gore so many years ago called the "inconvenient truth" about what it will take to save our planet—will we be able to take action to halt or mitigate the destruction.

None of what's happening now comes as a surprise. Scientists have been predicting this for years. In 1965, climate scientists Roger Revelle, Wallace Broecker, and others wrote in a paper to President Lyndon Johnson that "[m]an is unwittingly conducting a vast geophysical experiment. Within a few generations he is burning the fossil fuels that slowly accumulated in the earth over the past 500 million years," emphasizing that "[t]he climatic changes that may be produced by the increased CO_2 content could be deleterious from the point of view of human beings. The possibilities of deliberately bringing about countervailing climatic changes therefore need to be thoroughly explored." The team predicted that, by the year 2000, we would see the melting of the Antarctic ice caps, rising sea levels, warming of the oceans, increased acidity of water, and other catastrophic events (Revelle, 1965).

Well, here we are.

The heatwave that rocked the Pacific Northwest with 100-degree days in 2022 was, sadly, not unexpected, and only the latest reminder that decades of slow and steady global warming is reaching a tipping point. The hottest year in human history officially entered the record books as 2023. To say that it's infuriating to see the can kicked down the road is an understatement—those 50-year-old predictions that stunned Johnson are now coming to pass—and it's clear that previous administrations chose to defer action on this issue rather than address it.

The Earth's climate is changing. Temperatures are rising, snow and rainfall patterns are shifting, and more extreme climate events—like heavy rainstorms and record-high temperatures—are already happening. Many of these observed changes are linked to the rising levels of carbon dioxide and other greenhouse gases in our atmosphere, caused by human activities.

The answers to prevent further disaster are clear: cut carbon emissions drastically and right away while also mitigating the damage caused by decades of willful ignorance. The sins of the past will be with us for centuries to come, but we have the tools and knowledge to prevent total disaster if we are willing to work together now. That involves convincing people that global warming is real.

Unfortunately, during President Trump's time in office, we lost four precious years to make substantial progress on the problem. He was neither willing nor prepared to address this issue or, at the very least, consistently acknowledge its existence. His dismissal of existing scientific data was dangerous for the citizens of this country for whom the effects of global warming are already at hand. Trump and his advisors politicized global warming, while Trump's ability to shift blame—projective identification in action—has altered how we communicate with each other, even though he's no longer in office. These behaviors have made it nearly impossible to have an open and honest dialogue about present and future environmental issues since even basic facts were called into question under Trump's presidency, such as whether global warming even exists. When facts are less important than ideology, there's little room left for finding a middle ground and even less hope of finding solutions, no matter where we fall in our political beliefs—we're all breathing the same air after all.

GOVERNMENT-LED INITIATIVES

After months of negotiation and vaulting the major hurdle of securing a "yes" vote from Senator Joe Manchin, climate legislation eventually passed the Senate in 2022. True, Manchin has significant ties to the oil and gas industries, and the Inflation Reduction Act (IRA) now includes significant concessions to those sectors, but let's focus on the good stuff, and there's a lot of it. The IRA allocates an eye-popping $369 billion in direct funding for initiatives that reduce carbon emissions and for investments in energy security, with $60 billion specifically earmarked for environmental justice and pollution mitigation in low-income communities.

According to the summary released by Senate Democrats, this law will "make a historic down payment on deficit reduction, fight inflation, invest in domestic energy production and manufacturing, and reduce carbon emissions by roughly 40 percent by 2030." Such a reduction isn't enough to stop global warming—recall that the planet is already 1.1 degrees Celsius warmer than it was a century ago—but the action has the potential to thwart the catastrophic outcomes predicted if nothing is done. Additionally, addressing the climate crisis cannot happen on the backs of a few countries; everyone needs to participate, and a recent UN (2022) report found that "[i]nnovation has lagged in developing countries due to weaker enabling conditions" (p. 15). Let's not kid ourselves; the road ahead is long and perilous, but this bill gives us a fighting chance.

Passed through budget reconciliation, meaning all 50 Democrats plus Vice President Harris voted for it, the IRA sailed through the House and was signed into law by President Biden on August 16, 2022.

Some critics say the concessions regarding oil and gas drilling negated the law's benefits, requiring that the federal government offer millions of on- and offshore land for oil and gas drilling before permitting offshore wind energy programs. But the 700-plus-page law is the largest single expenditure to address the climate crisis in American history and encompasses incentives for industries to shift quickly to green jobs and technologies. And just because the federal government must now offer these lands for lease doesn't mean companies will buy and drill; the land must only be offered for sale. According to reporting by *High Country News*, "the government has put an average of 4.4 million acres per year on the block" since 2009, but "only 1.3 million of those acres, on average, received bids" (Thompson, 2022). Most bidders wanted the land to beef up their portfolios to attract investors. So, no, it's not perfect, but it's not quite the "climate suicide pact" some progressives claim it to be.

Republicans, meanwhile, are bemoaning the tiny tax increase, but more than 25% of the new cash will derive from funding the Internal Revenue Service (IRS) to actually enforce existing tax code. Former vice chairman of the Federal Reserve Alan Blinder wrote in *The Wall Street Journal* that injecting the IRS with a much-needed cash infusion will allow it to collect "more of what Congress has already legislated" and that "[y]ou'll probably need a magnifying glass to see any damage to investment or jobs, and any damages will surely be dwarfed by the bill's job-creating provisions on climate change and prescription jobs."

And one year in, the White House estimates that the IRA is already making changes by creating more than 170,000 clean energy jobs and encouraging companies to invest $110 billion in clean energy manufacturing. We need more time to do this work (White House, 2023).

Even commentary in the Murdoch-owned beacon of capitalism

hasn't kept some Republican lawmakers from suggesting that climate change is a leftist hoax designed to encourage a socialist takeover of the United States—and this despite billions of dollars in the IRA allocated for business development. Still others argue that accepting climate change would allow an elite international cabal to impose crippling sanctions and infringe on the sovereignty of the nation. This is a common refrain among populists here and abroad who successfully created the climate-crisis bogeyman to sow unnecessary fear and paranoia among the populace, but it is nothing more than a ruse—a powerful one, at that—to convince people that the climate crisis is a joke and they should only trust elected officials willing to fight the vast conspiracy. In truth, these are ploys designed to manipulate frightened people and to wrangle power for themselves.

Yet facts are facts, and the climate crisis is wreaking so much havoc on red and blue states (look to flooding in Kentucky, triple-digit temperatures from coast to coast, and rivers so dry people can walk across them) that the word "catastrophic" feels almost overused when describing these circumstances.

Further, fully two thirds of Americans—a statistic that includes many Republicans—think government isn't doing enough to address climate change. Fully 92% of Democrats and 88% of Republicans favor planting "about a trillion trees around the world to absorb carbon emissions in the atmosphere." Even climate-crisis denier-in-chief Donald Trump advocated for tree planting efforts in his 2020 State of the Union address.

So, where does that leave us?

Until recently, climate change was slow and abstract: It's been awfully hard to encourage people and governments to enact policies meant to prevent climate disasters when the pace of change seemed incremental or invisible (Cunsolo & Ellis, 2018). Winters with slightly less snow? No big deal, until 30 years go by, and residents of traditionally snow-covered terrain find themselves with mud instead. This kind of slow or invisible change is hard to mourn in real time and also makes it challenging to mobilize efforts to combat it. If you can't see it, it's hard to get upset about it.

Until you do. Until the day a farmer wakes up to fields inundated with river water. When fires burn so hot that they spawn their own weather systems. When a spring morning is eerily bereft of birdsong. When there's more plastic in the ocean than fish.

Remember that motivational Westinghouse poster of Rosie the Riveter, sleeve rolled, arm bared, ready to take on the challenges of war on the home front? We need to channel that resolve if we will make any positive progress against the climate crisis. And women must be prepared to lead this battle. Perhaps Barbie can help lead the way.

MAY YOU LIVE IN TROUBLING TIMES

And so we do—from threats to democracy on various fronts, wealth and racial inequality, and the rapid heating of the planet, it's hard to know where to look first. I contend that an uninhabitable globe renders most other issues meaningless. We have the tools and the ingenuity to mitigate the massive earthly problems requiring human intervention.

Most governments are simply not doing enough—nor have they for the past, oh, 50 years—so while it would be nice to see more from our elected leaders than meaningless platitudes and the touting of tiny achievements as monumental (though every little bit does help), we've got to look to our NGOs, our community leaders, and our captains of industry to take up the charge.

Women will be the deciding factor in whether anything much happens at all levels, but especially at the ground level.

Women, on the whole, experience climate change differently and more profoundly than men. According to a report from the UN (2022), "[w]omen are increasingly…more vulnerable than men to the impacts of climate change, mainly because they represent the majority of the world's poor and are proportionally more dependent on threatened natural resources." The report also reveals that women generally have less access than men to tools like credit, technology, and basic education—tools that would help women—and, in turn, the rest of humanity—adapt to the changing climate (Balsha, 2009).

Of the 1.3 billion people in the world living in poverty, 70% are women. Women produce most of the world's food, yet they own hardly 10% of all land. Women shoulder the burden of nourishing the world, are the first to feel the consequences of extreme weather events, and are, by and large, woefully underprepared to adapt. If the world's women fail, we're doomed. As one activist puts it, "If you are invisible in everyday life, your needs will not be thought of, let alone addressed, in a crisis situation" (UN, 2022).

Advancing equality for women doesn't require decreasing our economic focus; by contrast, a 2015 McKinsey & Company report found that "$12 trillion could be added to global GDP by 2025 by advancing women's equality" (Woetzel et al., 2015). Raising women's cultural and economic profile helps everyone and can help our planet. A significant change would be to grant more women land rights. In a May 2022 speech, the Under-Secretary of the United Nations, Sima Bahous, made the compelling case for granting more land rights to women: "Women's land rights are intrinsically and vitally linked to gender equality. They are key enablers of women's economic autonomy and decision-making. They are a major factor in rebalancing unequal power relations within homes, communities, and institutions" (Bahous, 2022).

Unfortunately, the pandemic hit women hard, and recovery has been intermittent. Initiatives like UN Women are gathering on-the-ground data and supporting programs to increase gender equality and access to land rights.

In many countries, long-held cultural beliefs prevent women from considering opportunities that would improve their lives and help the environment. Empowering women is an important step, but it's necessary to help the rest of the community understand why such drastic change can yield wide-ranging benefits—and this is where I believe mental health professionals have much to offer. No matter how much we may tell people that doing X is good for their health or the planet, so often that well-intentioned advice falls on deaf ears. To create change, we've got to help people into the right mindset—to see change as something they are actively engaged in, not as something forced on them. Community-wide psychological empowerment can be that catalyst for increased awareness of how global events touch our lives while providing encouragement that we have the strength to make positive changes in our own lives.

Large initiatives are crucial, but so are the small, mundane efforts undertaken daily by ordinary people. We can find out what our local politicians and business leaders are doing to reduce carbon pollution and ensure gender equity. The group Count Us In at www.count-us-in.org provides language on how to go about this.

Barbie is ready to tackle this crisis, and like her, I know we're ready to roll up our sleeves and do the work. It's easy to feel overwhelmed by the enormity of the task. Choose a cause that's dear to you, and devote yourself to it. Each of us doing one thing is better than most of us doing nothing.

SOLASTALGIA AND THE CLIMATE-MENTAL HEALTH CRISIS

Is it the Apocalypse yet? Every time I turn on the news, flames appear to engulf another part of the world. Even the coral isn't safe! I'm starting to lose hope.

Reader, I am sharing this not to frighten you or send you into an existential depression. Instead, I share this because I suspect many of us, especially *our patients*, feel these same emotions—feelings of angst, despair, helplessness, and anger. Let us imagine that Barbie feels these emotions, too.

The changing climate will continue to influence our lives in negative ways—I don't think there's any way around that—but the psychological community must double down on its efforts to *identify* and *treat* mental health disorders caused by a warming planet.

Here are a few things we can do to help people like the reader who shared the concern above:

- Try to use neutral language when describing the changing climate. For example, discussing the *climate crisis* may produce greater anxiety than discussing a *changing climate*.
- Encourage patients to *accept* that the climate is changing. Acceptance is an important early step toward processing the various emotions that come with eco-grief and allows for cultivating resilience.
- Studies show women bear more significant impacts from climate change. Join initiatives to empower women with the tools and resources to adapt.
- Remind patients that individual action can make positive change.
- Recognize the difference between environmental grief and environmental anxiety. *Environmental grief* includes feelings of sadness that so much destruction has already happened that it causes the patient to go into a type of mourning. Patients suffering from *environmental anxiety* tend to exhibit more fear for the future and a sense of paralysis with how to cope.

Fifty years ago, psychoanalyst Howard F. Searles was one of the few sounding the alarm on the consequences of unchecked interference with the delicate balance of the natural world. He pioneered psychiatric study and the intimate, inextricable link between humans and the natural world. Even in 1972, Searles recognized the devastation the impending climate crisis would mean for our collective mental health. Though his work did not reach a wide audience right away, it has become, sadly, more relevant in the intervening years.

Climate change is real. It's here, and it's killing us and other life on our planet. Climate change doesn't care whether you're Republican or Democrat. But it's understandable if many Americans feel overwhelmed with the enormity of the task we face. It is easy to take a nihilist approach—that nothing we do matters, so we might as well go down singing. (One could argue that some members of the Republican Party are taking such a position.) But, for others, such an attitude only makes those horrible feelings of guilt and helplessness unbearable. We are all negatively affected by this crisis, and this is another facet of eco-grief.

Mourn what we've lost—and there's plenty that's gone forever—but I urge Americans to proceed with hope and find some ways, no matter how small, to get involved in healing ourselves and our planet. Eschewing plastic, eating vegetarian, or shopping local can feel almost feeble in the face of the challenges ahead, but every effort we make is significant and creates forward motion.

REGRET, ANXIETY, AND CLIMATE CHANGE DENIAL

Psychoanalyst Sally Weintrobe is a pioneer in the field of climate psychology. In 2012, she edited *Engaging with Climate Change*, in which sociologists, academics, and psychoanalysts offered diverse perspectives on the human response to climate change. Her latest book, *The Psychological Roots of the Climate Crisis*, examines the "culture of uncare," a system she argues "works to sever our felt caring links with the environment and with each other" (2021). By examining the origins of the disavowal of the global climate crisis, Weintrobe hopes to spark discussion among readers of various backgrounds and remains hopeful that humankind can save itself.

She suggests that the last half century has been beset by governments whose economies and political ideology have worked to deregulate the human mind to fit better with economic progress—an unbalancing of the human mind in the service of economic gain. Weintrobe looks to literary inspiration for this unbalancing, specifically in Ayn Rand's 1957 *Atlas Shrugged*, a neoliberal celebration of exceptionalism supporting the theory that "selfishness is admirable" (Weintrobe, 2021).

Protagonist Hank Rearden, a successful industrialist, is held up as the model for entrepreneurial grit: "I refuse to apologize for my ability—I refuse to apologize for my success—I refuse to apologize for my money," he asserts. Weintrobe argues that people like Rearden are paranoid about sharing their hard-earned gains with workers. As such, these Hank-Rearden types feel "unappreciated and resentful and go to extreme lengths to vilify anyone who may question either their wealth or ask for help."

Bringing this back to the climate crisis, Weintrobe suggests that, like Rearden, ultra-right-wing billionaires and conservative politicians will pull out all the stops and indulge in fantastic propaganda to prevent entities from enacting environmental policies that may result in diminished economic returns.

Despite the odds, Weintrobe sees light at the end of the dark tunnel. "People are reacting to climate reality in two main ways, trying to either avoid it or accept it (and mostly probably struggling between the two)," she writes. The climate crisis is a collective trauma; eventually, we will all feel its consequences. Part of the healing process is to ask for forgiveness—of the earth, of those who have felt the crisis firsthand—and then to work together to find solutions.

It is important to be positive about our chances, but we must also move quicker than we have. Species are disappearing and environments are becoming less hospitable to supporting life. We can enact change, but it must come soon. To that end, I offer the final lines of a poem of regret by Carl Sandburg entitled "Buffalo Dusk" to remind us that once something's gone, it's merely a memory:

> *The buffaloes are gone.*
> *And those who saw the buffaloes are gone. (Sandburg, 1970)*

REFERENCES

Bahous, S. (2022, May 24). *Speech: Women's land rights are intrinsically and vitally linked to gender equality.* UN Women – Headquarters. https://www.unwomen.org/en/news-stories/speech/2022/05/speech-womens-land-rights-are-intrinsically-and-vitally-linked-to-gender-equality?utm_campaign=Dr.+Karyne+Messina%27s+Newsletter&utm_medium=email&utm_source=Revue+newsletter

Blinder, A. (2022, August 4). GOP frets over the inflation reduction act's tiny tax increase. *Wall Street Journal.* *https://www.wsj.com/articles/republicans-fret-over-inflation-reduction-acts-tiny-tax-increase-recession-budget-agreement-supply-demand-economic-growth-11659644730?utm_campaign=Dr.%20Karyne%20Messina%27s%20Newsletter&utm_medium=email&utm_source=Revue%20newsletter*

Cunsolo, A., & Ellis, N. (2018, April). Ecological grief as a mental health response to climate-change related loss. *Nature 8,* 275–281. https://www.nature.com/articles/s41558-018-0092-2.epdf?author_access_token=UJYCnlw0zZieuYACw3AJQtRgN0jAjWel9jnR3ZoTv0MZ8cLxe72VDW0esMFb0zEFM26k9KCrjCPa-wqxJcwmMgcIei5y7ci3SN_gtpLunMyI9r_Qst3A5V3rz96ScHSGy2dP3IB1DKK9qNem8yIrw%3D%3D

Davenport, C. (2020, November 9). What will Trump's most profound legacy be? Possibly climate damage. *The New York Times.* Retrieved January 23, 2024, from https://www.nytimes.com/2020/11/09/climate/trump-legacy-climate-change.html

Elasha, B. O. (2009). *Women… in the shadow of climate change.* United Nations. https://www.un.org/en/chronicle/article/womenin-shadow-climate-change?utm_campaign=Dr.+Karyne+Messina%27s+Newsletter&utm_medium=email&utm_source=Revue+newsletter

Kapfunde, M. (2019, April 11). *How ecoBirdy found a solution to the 80 percent of plastic toys that end up in a landfill.* FashNerd. https://fashnerd.com/2018/05/ecobirdy-sustainable-recycling-innovative-technology/#:~:text=According%20to%20ecoBirdy's%20website%2C%2080,just%20six%20months%20on%20average

Lange, J. (2023, July 21). *The dubious sustainability of eco Barbies.* Heatmap News. https://heatmap.news/culture/barbie-plastics-recycled-eco-leadership

Leopold, A. S. (1949). *A Sand County Almanac and sketches here and there… illustrated by Charles W. Schwartz.* Oxford University Press.

Mattel. (n.d.). *Mattel playback and sustainability: Mattel.* Mattel Shop. https://shop.mattel.com/pages/playback

Nature Conservancy. (n.d.). *Our priorities: Tackle climate change.* The Nature Conservancy. https://www.nature.org/en-us/what-we-do/our-priorities/tackle-climate-change/

Revelle, R., Broecker, W., et al. (1965, November). *Restoring the quality of our environment: report of the environmental pollution panel.* The President's Science Advisory Committee. The White House. https://carnegiedge.s3.amazonaws.com/downloads/caldeira/PSAC,%201965,%20Restoring%20the%20Quality%20of%20Our%20Environment.pdf

Ruffin, D. (2024, January 20). *Is life in plastic recyclable after all? The aftermath of Barbie.* Plastic Reimagined. https://www.plasticreimagined.org/articles/is-life-in-plastic-fantastic-after-all-the-aftermath-of-barbie

Sandburg, C. (1970). *The complete poems of Carl Sandburg.* Harcourt Brace Iovanovich Inc.

Schlanger, Z. (2023, December 4). *The climate can't afford another trump presidency. The Atlantic.* Retrieved January 23, 2024, from https://www.theatlantic.com/magazine/archive/2024/01/trump-climate-change-denial-paris-agreement/676125/

Schmidt, A. (2020, March 9). *Barbie by the numbers: What to know about the iconic Doll's history.* Fox Business. https://www.foxbusiness.com/lifestyle/barbie-by-numbers

Thompson, J. (2022, August 5). *Climate game changer? Or fossil fuel giveaway?* High Country News. https://www.hcn.org/articles/analysis-climate-change-climate-game-changer-or-suicide-pact/

UN. (2022, February 28). *Explainer: How gender inequality and climate change are interconnected.* UN Women – Headquarters. Explainer: How gender inequality and climate change are interconnected | UN Women – Headquarters.

Weintrobe, S. (2021). *Psychological roots of the climate crisis: Neoliberal exceptionalism and the culture of uncare.* New York: Bloomsbury Academic.

The White House. (2023, August 16). FACT SHEET: One year in, President Biden's Inflation Reduction Act is driving historic climate action and investing in America to create good paying jobs and reduce costs. *The White House.* Retrieved from https://www.whitehouse.gov/briefing-room/statements-releases/2023/08/16/fact-sheet-one-year-in-president-bidens-inflation-reduction-act-is-driving-historic-climate-action-and-investing-in-america-to-create-good-paying-jobs-and-reduce-costs/

Woetzel, L., Madgavkar, A., Ellingrud, K., Labaye, E., Devillard, S., Kutcher, E., Manyika, J., Dobbs, R., & Krishnan, M. (2015). (report). *How advancing women's equality can add $12 trillion to global growth.* McKinsey & Co. Retrieved from https://www.mckinsey.com/featured-insights/employment-and-growth/how-advancing-womens-equality-can-add-12-trillion-to-global-growth?utm_campaign=Dr.%20Karyne%20Messina%27s%20Newsletter&utm_medium=email&utm_source=Revue%20newsletter

Woody, T. (2022, October 21). *Mattel remakes Barbie with recycled plastic.* Bloomberg.com. https://www.bloomberg.com/news/features/2022-10-21/mattel-remakes-barbie-with-recycled-plastic

Essay Five

The Original Identity Crisis in America

Exploitation Nation Pre-Barbie

The concept of America's singular identity has been challenged by its complex history of colonization and displacement of Indigenous populations. Indigenous peoples inhabited and stewarded the American continent for millennia before the arrival of Europeans, developing rich cultures and complex societies that existed in harmony with the natural environment. European colonization resulted in the dispossession and marginalization of Indigenous communities, disrupting their way of life and causing immense suffering. The introduction of foreign diseases in particular had devastating consequences for Indigenous populations, contributing to significant loss of life and cultural disruption.

The original American identity crisis is far from over, a complex situation that we can better understand by examining the legacies of the past. Understanding the historical roots of this crisis can foster more informed and constructive conversations about who we are as a nation and what values we want to uphold.

Further, I believe we must approach this topic with sensitivity and avoid generalizations as much as possible, since the experiences and attitudes of white Americans of European descent are diverse and not monolithic. However, we can explore some harmful patterns of projection and projective identification by white Americans onto white women, Indigenous peoples, and black Americans. These acts led to our country's current identity crisis as well as the mistreatment and exploitation of various ethnic groups.

WHITE WOMEN IN COLONIAL AMERICA

In the new world, experiences of the newcomers varied greatly from colony to colony, mainly for women and children. Treatment also depended on social status and ethnic background. In the South, women settlers were often treated like indentured servants. In fact, many early white colonists were impoverished, illiterate, indentured servants. As such, it is challenging to generalize what all women may have experienced in colonial America, especially as it pertains to their identities. But there are some universal factors that likely shaped their sense of self.

Most European societies were entrenched patriarchies that limited female agency and representation. Regardless of where they lived, white women in colonial America had many responsibilities. They oversaw managing the household, including baking, sewing, educating children, and producing home goods. Mortality rates were high, the land was harsh and unfamiliar, and women were expected to help keep the communities afloat while generally deferring to their husbands or fathers (Berkin, 1997).

As members of a growing middle class in the 18th century, some women became assistants to their husbands as innkeepers or traders. These added responsibilities did not come with additional benefits; women were still considered second-class citizens with the rights to match. Any improvements in social status were superficial, as women continued to live as subordinates to men (Lerner, 1986, p. 217). Why not just throw off the shackles of the past and embrace a new identity in the new world? Patriarchy exists thanks to deeply held beliefs that women are inferior to men. On a psychological level, most women believed that (and many today still do). Patriarchy only functions if both men and women believe it. Changing those beliefs on a society-wide level can take decades, if ever. Merely pulling up stakes and moving across the Atlantic or across the western Plains does not change the fundamental psychological underpinnings that uphold patriarchies.

Even though we are a long way from those early uncertain colonial days, as we explored in Essay Two, patriarchies don't just fade away, and seeds that were planted in the early days of our country took root and influence how men and women think about themselves today.

WESTWARD EXPANSION

During westward expansion, settlers got bolder and took more and more land from American Indians, which meant killing (either directly or indirectly) the Indigenous people living there. According to a report that appeared in *Quaternary Science Reviews*, European settlers killed 56 million Indigenous people in the Americas. That bloodshed changed the global climate—land that had been used for farming purposes by Indigenous peoples reverted to forests, which in turn decreased the amount of carbon dioxide in the atmosphere (Koch et al., 2019).

Carnage of humans and of animals in the New World benefited the Europeans. This slaughter allowed Europeans to leave a life of hardship behind for a fresh start in North America. Eventually, Americans of European descent came to believe that they were superior to people whose ancestors were here before the arrival of Europeans. Some European-Americans came to believe that they were "pureblood" and "more American" than their non-European counterparts. This sense of superiority contributed to the creation of an inflated sense of cultural identity. However, we *all* came from mixed stock. Despite our own humble beginnings, Americans feel special if they can lay claim to *Mayflower* ancestors. However, the people on that ship were hardly special. They were servants, children, Pilgrim separatists, non-separatists, and women, none of whom were part of the "upper crust" of England.

In the 19th century, the phrase "Manifest Destiny" was frequently used to describe the deeply held belief among white Americans that it was their destiny to expand across America. The journalist John L. O'Sullivan advocated for the annexation of Oregon in an 1845 article for the *New York Morning News* with the now-famous phrase "that the claim is by the right of our manifest destiny to overspread and to possess the whole of the continent which Providence has given us for the development of the great experiment of liberty and federated self-government entrusted to us" (Pratt, 1933). This sentiment reveals that westward expansion was believed to have been readily apparent and unavoidable—that there was a special virtue associated with the United States existing as a country and that it was white America's heavenly ordained mission to fulfill this mission.

A documentary produced by Ken Burns in 2023 focuses on the harrowing experiences of the Indigenous people as well as of the American bison, one that historian Rosalyn LaPier describes as two distinct tales. One is a chronicle of the intimate relationship between Indigenous communities and the buffalo, a bond nurtured over millennia. The other is the darker story of the buffalo's near annihilation at the hands of European settlers and the subsequent Americans.

These settlers, driven by cash bounties for buffalo hides—greed again—decimated the buffalo population, causing it to plummet from 30 million to less than 1,000 within a few decades. This massacre spelled calamity for the Indigenous tribes, whose existence was intertwined with the buffalo. In what Burns views as a concerted effort, this annihilation not only targeted the buffalo, but also fulfilled an unofficial policy that killing buffalo would kill the Indigenous peoples (Kimbrough, 2023). The near extinction of the buffalo is a bloody reminder that ecosystems and identity are intertwined, and the decimation of these animals coincided with the deliberate killing of Indigenous peoples and the systematic destruction of their traditions and communities.

STRIPPED IDENTITY

A terrible tale of stripped identity and murder of Osage Indians in Oklahoma remained unfamiliar to most Americans until recently. This gruesome fact only came to light in recent years when journalist David Grann visited an Osage museum and saw a photo of Osage members and white settlers hanging on a wall. He noticed that a part of the picture was missing, like it had been intentionally ripped. When he inquired about the photo, he was told part of it was removed because it was too frightening. This idea stuck in Grann's mind when he realized it was part of history that wasn't part of any public record. This omission led Grann to write the powerful *Killers of the Flower Moon*, which finally told the story of how land was stolen from the Osage people of Oklahoma (Grann, 2017). (It turned out that the missing part of the photo includes one of the men who killed Osage women.)

During the 1890s, the Osage Nation sidestepped the allotment system devised by the US government to remove Indigenous people from their land, but the Osage approved the Allotment Bill in 1906, around the same time that oil was discovered on their land. There was so much oil that it made Oklahoma residents the wealthiest people per capita in the world.

A common misconception among white Americans at the time was that Indigenous people weren't sophisticated and needed guidance, especially when it came to financial decisions. This was hardly the case, but white Americans stepped in under this pretense to set systems in place that would allow them to steal from the Osage.

The Osage tribal leadership parceled 657 acres of land to each member. These parcels included mineral rights, meaning each Osage legally owned any valuable minerals found beneath the surface of his or her land, which, in this case, could be oil. Neoliberalism was not an Osage quality. Instead of every man and woman being out for him or herself, each member of the group shared in the wealth of the land.[11]

The only way land could transfer between owners was through marriage or inheritance. Many white American men came to Oklahoma and married Osage women, who often turned up dead after their nuptials were official. Many murders were unreported, and few were ever solved. Despite this lack of justice, the Osage survived and retained knowledge of their culture and identiy.

> The modern day Osage is educated, diverse and staunch to the fact that being Osage is their identity. Our native culture today is a respectful memorial to our past. We participate in our dance, our feasting and our naming ceremonies because that is what we have left. We do not try to re-create the past, we are the present and our culture is in the present. (Oklahoma State Department of Education, 2014)

THE TRAGEDY IN TULSA AND WHY THE GREENWOOD NEIGHBORHOOD WAS DESTROYED

Oklahoma was a rough place at the turn of the 20th century. A decade after the Osage murders, as many as 300 people were killed in Tulsa in one of the deadliest race massacres in US history. This horrific

---

11. After the government passed a law requiring the Osage members to prove they were competent to manage their money, they were assigned a guardian who stole approximately $8,000,000 from them. In today's world, that would be equivalent to approximately $125,628,360.

event appeared to occur as a result of a rumor about a Black man raping a white woman which lead an angry white mob to destroy many acres of a prosperous Black neighborhood. However, it was later determined that the area exploded because of a combination of kerosene and nitroglycerine. Did white Americans actively decide to reject the Constitution's own principles of forming a perfect union? Is this because Americans of European descent have no real identity, meaning they stand up for what they say they believe in when it is convenient and don't when the truth is inconvenient? Do identity and perception have two sides? For example, the official transmitted history says one thing ("scary," "unruly" Black residents rioting, with "good" white residents saving the city) while truth reveals destructive, envious and murderous impulses.

HOW IT ALL BEGAN IN TULSA

Oklahoma was ratified as a state in 1907. At that point, O.W. Gurley, one of the world's richest Black men, bought land in Tulsa and opened a boarding house and a grocery store. He sold land to other Black people, who bought homes and established profitable businesses in the Greenwood section of the city, creating what came to be known as "Black Wall Street," a hugely successful black business district. While successful from a business perspective, Tulsa remained bound to Jim Crow laws that denied Black Americans the right to vote, the ability to seek certain jobs, and access to certain educational opportunities.

As was the case with the Osage Nation, many white men in America couldn't tolerate the success of Black people. Using a false allegation of the rape of a white woman (Sarah Page) by Dick Rowland, a 19-year-old Black man, a mob of white rioters—some of whom had been deputized by the police department—looted and burned Greenwood to the ground.

Contemporary historians estimate that 300 people died over a two-day period. No one was ever charged with a crime.

INFORMATION FROM THE 2001 RACE RIOT COMMISSION REPORT

After the Tulsa massacre, Black residents believed Dick Rowland would be lynched for what allegedly happened to Sarah Page. They thought they had to protect themselves because of what happened to their homes and businesses. Members of the community thought they could only count on themselves. "As hostile groups gathered and their confrontation worsened, municipal and county authorities failed to take actions to calm or contain the situation (*1921 Tulsa Race Massacre – Tulsa Historical Society & Museum*, 2022)."

The Greenwood residents guessed correctly; after local authorities deputized as many white men as possible, racial violence became a state-sanctioned activity, and each new deputy received firearms and ammunition.

PROJECTION, PROJECTIVE IDENTIFICATION, AND/OR BLAME SHIFTING

To add insult to injury, Black detainees could only be released from Tulsa jails if a white person applied for their release. This is similar to when the Osage people were forced into financial "guidance" when it came to spending their own money—it is another example of projection, projective identification, and/or blame shifting. White people committed the crimes but consciously or unconsciously had to mentally get rid of any negative thoughts or feelings about themselves. Since they apparently couldn't consider the possibility that they had broken the law, they projected the "badness" or criminal acts onto black people who had been victimized. The Tulsa Massacres were rebranded as riots that began in Greenwood and had to be tamed by white vigilantes/deputies to save the city. They then watched and controlled them to make sure the accused were still considered guilty so no one would suspect that they were the ones who were the villainous perpetrators. This maneuver worked since not one of these criminal actors have ever been prosecuted by the government at any level: municipal, county, state, or federal. Even after the restoration of order, it was official policy to release a black detainee only if a white person applied and agreed to accept responsibility for that detainee's subsequent behavior.

Not all white Tulsa residents were complicit in these killings; some white neighbors shared invaluable assistance with the massacre victims, and the American Red Cross served as a model of human compassion. Although city and county government bore much of the cost for Red Cross relief, neither contributed substantially to Greenwood's rebuilding. In fact, municipal authorities acted initially to impede rebuilding, but that did not deter the residents, who rebuilt their neighborhood and their businesses almost immediately after the massacres. Greenwood thrived for another 45 years until the construction of the Crosstown Expressway, which bisected the Greenwood District and put an end to the renaissance of Black Wall Street (Moreno, 2021).

In the same way the Osage people knew who they were as a nation, the people of Black Wall Street did as well. Both groups were stripped of their dignity and of their identity because their success conflicted with dominant narratives about white supremacy.

MASS GRAVE INVESTIGATIONS

As mentioned, no one was ever held accountable for what happened in Greenwood. Allegations of bodies being dumped in mass graves circulated almost as soon as the smoke cleared. None of those murders would be investigated until 2020 under the direction of Republican mayor G.T. Bynum. "[M]y family were white people who lived here in 1921. I'm not trying to make white people look bad. I'm just trying to find the truth," Bynum said in an interview with *The Washington Post*.

Like many other Americans, Bynum had never heard of the Tulsa Massacre, and he certainly did not self-identify as a racist, but rediscovering this sordid moment in his city's history is an important step towards repairing the damage of the past and understanding the community's collective trauma: "I'm not here to defend anything wrong the city has ever done on this," Bynum said. "We will follow the truth where that takes us" (Brown, 2020).

HOW CASTE SYSTEMS SHAPE IDENTITY

In *Caste: The Origins of Our Discontents*, Isabel Wilkerson described the caste system of categorizing people as "an artificial construction, a fixed and embedded ranking of human value that sets the presumed supremacy of one group against the presumed inferiority of other groups on the basis of ancestry and often immutable traits, traits that would be neutral in the abstract but are ascribed life-and-death meaning in a hierarchy favoring the dominant caste whose forebears designed it" (Wilkerson, 2020). Arbitrary boundaries established by the caste system allow hierarchies to remain fixed and function, in some cases, for millennia by exploiting and dehumanizing people who make up the lower rungs of the established order (Wilkerson, 2020, pp. 40–41).

To her categories of castes, I would add the Indigenous people of the Americas since they were also "victims of European conquest and/ or various forms of emotional, psychological, and cultural domination. Initially said colorism was maintained and carried out via threat of violence where all manner of European ideology was cast in the idealization of Whiteness via light skin" (Brown et. al, 2018).

Growing up within a caste system exposes individuals to messages about their worth and limitations. By hearing these messages repeatedly, people eventually (and unconsciously) internalize these beliefs about themselves. These identities are transmitted from one generation to the next, making it incredibly difficult for someone to break free from these deeply held beliefs.

THE ATROCITIES OF STRIPPING AWAY THE IDENTIFY OF OTHERS CONTINUES

Europeans became masters of the American continent by massacring Indians and enslaving Africans. The white man prior to the American colonists also wanted gold and other riches that were gathered by people they thought to be lowlier than they while totally disregarding the rights of these people.

One reason is that people foist onto others what they can't tolerate in themselves. Other reasons appear to be envy, greed, and the need for power, which is why neoliberal capitalism in one form or another has been in play for thousands of years. The absence of love seems to offer yet another explanation. If you can't have love, the next best thing appears to be power in many cases. Therein may lie the reason for the apparent sadism that exists in the world—not among all people but among many.

When all is said and done, it also may be the lack of an identity, of not knowing who one is and what one wants from life, that may be a key factor in having a meaningful life. Perhaps the most pervasive form of projection is the erasure or invisibility of Indigenous peoples. When their history, contributions, and voices are ignored or marginalized, it allows the dominant white narrative to remain unchallenged. This can contribute to a sense of entitlement and lack of awareness among white Americans regarding Indigenous identity and rights.

REFERENCES

1921 Tulsa Race Massacre – Tulsa Historical Society & Museum. Tulsa Historical Society & Museum. (2022, November 3). https://www.tulsahistory.org/exhibit/1921-tulsa-race -massacre/#flexible-content

Berkin, C. (1997). *First generations: Women in colonial America*. Hill and Wang.

Brown, D., Branden, K., & Hall, R. E. (2018). Native American colorism: From historical manifestations to the current era. *American Behavioral Scientist, 62*(14), 2023–2036. https://doi.org/10.1177/0002764218810751

Brown, D. (2020, March 13). A white Republican mayor seeks the truth about Tulsa's race massacre a century ago. *The Washington Post*. Retrieved from https://www .washingtonpost.com/history/2020/03/13/tulsa-mayor-bynum-mass-graves/

Grann, D. (2017, May 17). *The true story of killers of the Flower Moon*. Atlas Obscura. https://www.atlasobscura.com/articles/osage-murders-photos-killers-of-flower-moon.

Kimbrough, L. (2023, October 4). *Ken Burns discusses heartbreak & hope of "The American Buffalo," his new documentary*. Mongabay Environmental News. https://news.mongabay .com/2023/10/ken-burns-discusses-hope-heartbreak-of-the-american-buffalo-his-new -documentary/

Koch, A., Brierley, C., Maslin, M. M., & Lewis, S. L. (2019). Earth system impacts of the European arrival and Great Dying in the Americas after 1492. *Quaternary Science Reviews, 207*, 13–36. https://doi.org/10.1016/j.quascirev.2018.12.004

Moreno, C. (2021, June 2). *Decades after the Tulsa Race Massacre, urban "renewal" sparked Black Wall Street's second destruction*. Smithsonian.com. https://www.smithsonianmag .com/history/black-wall-streets-second-destruction-180977871/

Oklahoma State Department of Education. (2014, July). The Osage Nation. Oklahoma City. https://sde.ok.gov/sites/ok.gov.sde/files/documents/files/Tribes_of_OK_ Education%20Guide_Osage_Nation.pdf

Pratt, J. W. (1933). John l. O'Sullivan and Manifest Destiny. *New York History, 14*(3), 213–234. http://www.jstor.org/stable/24470589

Wilkerson, I. (2020). *Caste: The origins of our discontents*. Random House. Kindle Edition.

Essay Six

The Effects of the American Identity Crisis

How Understanding Projective Identification, Mentalization, Reparative Leadership, and How Truth and Reconciliation Commissions Work Could Make a Difference

> *By giving voice to the cognitive dissonance required to be a woman under the patriarchy, you robbed it of its power.*
> —BARBIE, the movie (2023)

In the excerpt above, stereotypical Barbie pinpoints how a brainwashed Barbie snapped out of a trance the Kens had conjured up when they imported patriarchy to Barbie Land. In the newly anointed Kendom, Barbies lose their identity and autonomy but are brought back to their senses by Gloria's speech about being a woman. The Barbie's regain their autonomy, see the error in matriarchy, and balance is restored.

If only the real world's problems of identity could be solved by a rousing monologue. Americans suffer from a crisis of identity and don't believe in themselves, their country, or their leaders. The essays in this book have attempted to examine how we got here by using Barbie and her world as our lodestar. Is there anything we can do to mitigate the effects of a society-wide identity crisis? Namely, can we regain our identities? The Barbies did it. If plastic playthings in an imaginary land can model a return to an identity, why can't we? We can, but it will require more than just words. We need the right combination of words plus the right mindsets and the right leaders to make a dent in the problem.

What we need is a way to repair the damage that we have done to each other.

There are four psychological processes that could help make our divided nation whole again. Understanding these four mechanisms could make a difference. Recognizing how a problem took shape is an important step toward healing. They include the taking back of projections thrust upon another person or group of people which occurs when *projective identification* is at play: *mentalization, reparative leadership*, and *truth and reconciliation* processes.

Here they are.

Projective identification is a major factor in the manipulation of others. It occurs when people try to obfuscate responsibility while shifting blame to innocent people. This is how it works: People who are acutely uncomfortable with a feeling or thought in any given circumstance have an unconscious urge to "get rid of it." When this internal sense arises, this individual or group of people will project it onto (some say "into") someone else. The receiver of these projected thoughts initially suspects that something odd has occurred but doesn't know quite what it is. The "sender," on the other hand, feels relief. What's more, the sender may fantasize about keeping track of the receiver. These fantasies let the sender stay connected to the dispelled thought—gone, but not forgotten, to use the cliché. Fantasies are another way for the sender to monitor or control the receiver. In the mind's eye of the projector, it is as if he or she shares one mind with the recipient of the cast-off feeling or thought rather than having two separate minds. (Previously in my work, I have referred to projective identification as the "one-mind theory.")

As I mention above, the receiver of the projection initially tends to be taken aback. Following these feelings of confusion, he or she can often start to identify with the thought or feeling that was sent his or her way. The sender, on the other hand, often experiences a sense of freedom, at least temporarily, since the undesirable quality now resides with someone else.

Projective identification occurs in the *Barbie* movie when Gloria, depressed about her job, hitting middle age, and having a strained relationship with her daughter, begins drawing weird and sad Barbies. Through the magic of film, these thoughts and feelings are projected onto Stereotypical Barbie back in Barbie Land. At the outset, Barbie is confused by these new feelings (thoughts of death pop into her head during a choreographed dance party), but eventually she believes that she is worthless. Mentalization helps bring her back. (I'll explain what this is shortly.)

In the real world, we see projective identification play out with bullies. For example, a bully might call someone a "loser." The person receiving this projection initially may feel confused. However, before long he or she often comes to feel like a worthless or defeated person. When this occurs, the receiver is identifying with the thought or feeling that the projector sought to dispel and disavow. The twist in this dynamic is the likelihood that at an earlier time someone made the bully feel like a loser. Since that is not a comfortable feeling, the bully wants to get rid of it, so he or she projects it onto someone else. Again, the projector will frequently monitor the person who received the projection because the projector wants to make sure that the "loser status" remains with the receiver of the projection.

Projective identification can happen to people at any time. It is particularly problematic for people who are emotionally, physically, or sexually abused. We see this mechanism play out on social media among teenagers. For example, one girl may claim that another girl has had sex with lots of boys in school and is promiscuous. If this is posted on social media, the victim will more than likely become upset. Initially, she may feel stunned by the accusation or feel that the girl who wrote those things was jealous. However, when she is shunned, laughed at, and dropped by a group of friends, the victim will more than likely begin to question herself, thinking she might be perceived as a slut because she is friendly with boys. She might feel down on herself, which can lead to depression. She also may lose her sense of identity. Depending on the situation, a more serious outcome could occur, such as feelings of uselessness and despair culminating in thoughts of suicide. Making suicidal gestures or even suicide attempts can result when severe depression emerges. A lot of this type of behavior happens without adult knowledge or in private corners of the internet, and so it is extremely difficult to track. Abuse of this nature may be well established by the time an adult learns about it.

The antidote that can restore one's previous state of mind and identity is to give back the projected thought or feeling to the original projector. It is as if one says, "No, this isn't about me, it's about you."

Mentalization is a technique that helps people improve relations with others. This is when two people or groups of people come to understand others in an *atmosphere of respect* without passing judgement. Mentalization sounds easy, but it is actually quite challenging for people to actively listen to one another when there's a disagreement.

Unfortunately, as mentioned earier, this term is unknown to most people, including therapists, unless they have had exposure to it in specialized training programs. However, it is an extremely important concept, one I have called the "two-minds process." It applies to two people (or many) who are able to share thoughts and feelings in a respectful way. When people *mentalize* while they are engaged in a dialogue, the perceptions of *both* individuals (or many people in the case of groups) are accepted and not judged. This does not imply agreement, but rather indicates that each person is free to have and express his or her own opinions without being judged by the other, i.e., both views are permitted. When people mentalize, they can have their own thoughts without being ridiculed. Person A does not try to force Person B to think as he or she thinks. When someone can mentalize, that individual does not try to force his or her version of what is "right" or "acceptable" onto another or others; *all* thoughts and ideas can coexist. We see this in the *Barbie* movie in the final scenes when Ken is finally able to listen to Barbie and tell her how he feels about their relationship and that she ignores him—that he only "exists within the warmth of [her] gaze." Barbie is finally in a position to understand Ken and change.

Reparative leadership as I am using the term involves Melanie Klein's "positions" or states of being. In the *paranoid-schizoid position*, people project intolerable aspects of themselves or their group onto others and then blame those people for their own wrongdoing. In the depressive position, Klein's second and healthier position, what has been *attributed to others* is now *owned*. Another way of thinking about this dynamic is to think about "giving back projections," which I briefly discussed earlier in this essay and in more detail in *Misogyny, Projective Identification and Mentalization: Social, Political and Psychoanalytic Manifestations* (Messina, 2019).

C. Fred Alford, a political scientist and Kleinian scholar, connected her ideas of repair that occur in the depressive position with concepts established by the Frankfort School that promote the "four Rs": remembrance, reparation, reformation, and reconciliation. These theories emerged after World War II. I quote my writing from the book cited in the previous paragraph on pages 122-123.

> a group of social theorists working post-WWII and post-Holocaust, using what he termed the "four Rs": "Remembrance of those who suffered; Reparation for their loss; Reformation of reason; and Reconciliation with nature.
>
> Notably, "remorse" is not on this list of key goals. In Alford's view, raw emotion, including regret for past actions, is not useful; rather, the commitment to look forward and devise new ways to act—while keeping the past in mind—are what make all the difference. Change is possible if one embarks on

remembering, repairing, reforming, and reconciling while keeping in mind the harm done to others past and present, and making amends for one's own errors in a thoughtful manner as one gradually reconciles with all aspects of what it means to be human. (Messina, 2019).

Truth and reconciliation councils have been attempted dozens of times over the last 50 years to varying degrees of success. The most well-known are the South African Truth and Reconciliation Council and one in Rwanda based on the South African model.

CANADA

The Truth and Reconciliation of Canada (TRC) was put together to attempt to recognize and make reparations for transgressions against the county's Indigenous people. Specifically, ths TRC was established in 2008 to evaluate the extent of the damage that had been done to children who were sent to Catholic residential schools. It was also charged with informing Canadians of their findings. After reviewing over 5 million documents and gathering thousands of witness and victim statements, the final report issued in 2015 estimated that 150,000 children attended residential schools during the 120 years of the schools' existence and found that over 3,000 died while in the state's care. Of the nearly 70,000 students still alive, over 30,000 had at one time or another made claims of sexual assault. The TRC concluded that these schools committed cultural genocide. Reparations seem appropriate, but how much? And to whom?

According to the Canadian 2022 budget, billions of dollars (CAD) have been allocated to "advance reconciliation, protect the environment, and build stronger and more inclusive communities across Canada" (Government of Canada; Crown-Indigenous Relations and

Northern Affairs Canada, 2022). It is too soon to say whether these reparations have reached victims and what impact those dollars and programs have had on repairing the damage. But the identities of the mistreated Indigenous students have been validated and recognized by the Canadian government, and that's an important step toward recovery.

TRUTH AND RECONCILIATION COMMISSION, (TRC), SOUTH AFRICA

The South African government formed a TRC in 1995 to help repair damage done during the period of apartheid. One goal was to uncover the truth: to acknowledge all the ugliness and death that occurred. Although some people wanted the group to find and prosecute offenders in the manner of the Nuremberg trials after World War II, the focus of the TRC remained on truth and reconciliation.

After Nelson Mandela was released from his 18-year prison term for resisting the 300-year-old apartheid government, an opportunity for change and putting an end to white supremacist rule finally emerged. After lengthy negotiations, a temporary constitution was enacted until a permanent one could be agreed upon and established. During this timeframe, one major unresolved issue was whether to hold trials for those who participated during Apartheid. Some people wanted President de Klerk to issue a blanket amnesty. Eventually, it was agreed that the first democratically elected government would decide the fate of those who committed crimes (Brittanica, 2018).

Newly elected president Nelson Mandela appointed Archbishop Desmond Tutu to be the chair and Alex Boraine to be the deputy chair of the commission wherein three committees were established.

This yearlong commission met with people from every corner of South Africa, from civil rights lawyers and religious leaders to victims, to determine accountability and whether granting amnesty was appropriate. Also, the commission only concerned itself with human rights abuses that took place between 1960 and 1994—putting the entire 300-year history of colonization and apartheid on trial would have been impossible and unlikely to yield tangible results. Victims provided thousands of statements about human rights violations, including torture, killings, and kidnappings.

At public hearings, victims testified about the acts of violence they were forced to endure. The commission also held several thousand amnesty hearings. While key features of the hearings included openness and transparency wherein people throughout the country were made aware of the terrible things that occurred during the apartheid years, not all top-level former military leaders cooperated, which led to conflicts that hampered progress.

Despite the challenges and problems that existed in the South African TRC, it led to the most sweeping changes of any reconciliation in modern history. One of the key factors that made it so important was the ability of the public to participate in the trial process since victims and perpetrators both talked about their experiences.

RWANDAN TRC

The TRC of South Africa was not perfect, but it set a new standard for truth-telling, the need for repair, and reconciliation, including compensation. This example was adopted by the Rwandans after the 1994 genocide that killed over eight hundred people in approximately 100 days. Although the work that was done around truth and reconciliation was not perfect, Rwanda has made tremendous progress toward healing and reconciliation in the last 30 years, and their TRC helped their communities move beyond seemingly insurmountable issues (Souli, 2020).

When considering the subtitle posed in Essay Six—"Would Understanding *Projective Identification, Mentalization, Reparative Leadership, and a Truth and Reconciliation Plan Make a Difference*—it is interesting to consider whether the United States needs a truth and reconciliation commission for the entire country. According to Sarah Souli, who was based in Greece when Politico wrote an article in 2020 that covered the Truth and Dignity Commission in Tunisia, if ever there were a time when the United States needed some type of truth and reconciliate agenda, it would seem to be now, but it doesn't yet appear like there is one on the horizon. In that same Politico piece, Souli explored whether such an endeavor is possible. More than likely, the idea has never been discussed in decision-making circles, and politicians are unlikely to support such a move.

WHAT ABOUT BARBIE, THE DOLL, AND THE MOVIE: HAS FAIR PLAY BEEN PART OF THE CREATION AND DEVELOPMENT OF THIS FANTASY? HAS IDENTITY BEEN RESTORED?

The answer to the Barbie identity question is also unclear, largely because she did not begin life as Ruth Handler's creation. She started out as a sassy, German, blonde comic strip character called Lilli. She had strong opinions and knew what she wanted in life.

BECOMING A DOLL

So, the doll currently known as Barbie with no personality of her own was actually Lilli, whose own distinctive, highly sexualized persona was hidden from American consumers. Interesting that Barbie retained the voluptuous proportions of Lili—a sexy body with the mind of an innocent young woman. There is something disturbing about that—it is akin to the sexualization of preteens and adolescents who do not understand the power of their bodies and body language.

Barbie was not a toy upon which girls could project their dreams; she was a cartoon character created to entertain men. Once in America, Lilli's reincarnation as Barbie presents a question in terms of authenticity since Ruth Handler said she named her after her daughter, Barbara, while Ann Ryan, the daughter of a former Mattel vice president has said that her late father—who held several pattens for the doll—named her after his wife, whose name was Barbie. Who is right? Are they both a little right? Can both Handler and Ryan claim responsibility for creating Barbie?

If you look at the players in the Lilli/Barbie controversy, there are many examples of *projective identification*. One was demonstrated by Ruth Handler, who didn't like the doll's backstory—that she had stolen Lilli—so she projected that identity into oblivion and simply created a new history for Barbie even though the German toy company that created Lilli sued Handler for theft.

Mentalization might have helped if Handler and Mattel sat at the negotiation table and worked out an amicable financial arrangement wherein the Handlers and Mattel purchased the rights to Lilli in a fair mannered way, giving credit to all the creators of the comic strip and to the German toymaker who spent his life in misery because his creation was stolen. In 1963, Mattel entered into a settlement with Greiner and Hausser. Mattel purchased the copyright and patent rights in 1964 (LA Times, 2023).

Reparative leadership applies here too. Even though no one went to war, the largest toymaker in the world stole the concept that made Mattel worth approximately $6.88 billion dollars.

The appropriation of Lilli is what happens when neoliberalism is at play. The big guy gets all the riches while the little old toymaker ended up a broken man. Barbie looked an awfully lot like Lilli. "I was outraged when I saw the doll," recalled Rolf Hausser, whose toy company created and sold the Lilli doll. "This was my Lilli with a different name. What had these people done? Had they stolen my doll? I didn't know what happened" (Blakemore, 2023).

Eventually, Hausser sued Mattel, but unfortunately, he didn't know just how big of a phenomenon the doll had become. Although Hausser was outraged, his brother convinced him that suing Mattel was the worst thing he could do. Hausser followed this advice but later regretted it.

Still not understanding how popular Barbie was in the US, and what a phenomenon she was about to become, he was desperate to save his own corner of the European toy market. But his brother Kurt, aware of the influence of the rival toy giant, persuaded him that taking Mattel to court would end in financial ruin for the smaller German company. Instead, he suggested that O&M Hausser sell the doll's patent—probably the worst thing the company could have done.

Although a later court case was initiated by the German company because they claimed the agreement was in English, which they didn't understand, and included fraudulent claims, the California court eventually sided with Mattel and the case was dropped.

While an actual truth and conciliation commission would not be what one would consider in a case between a toymaker, Rolf Hausser, and a very large corporation such as the Mattel Corporation, some principles of human decency apply to this case.

Rolf Hausser died a downtrodden and likely very depressed man. It seemed as though his spirit was crushed by a huge neoliberal American company that showed no concern for the people and the doll that put them on the map. Given that Mattel has a net worth of approximately $6.88 billion, Hausser wasn't given a fair deal by any stretch of the imagination.

Further, despite what Mattel claims about corporate generosity, their CEO made $31.3 million a year in 2018, which was 4,987 times the amount of the median salary for employees globally at $6,271 (Cherney, 2018). Given those figures, perhaps a corporate truth and reconciliation group may be a reasonable thing to consider (Stewart, 2018).

REFERENCES

Alford, C. F. (1989). *Melanie Klein and critical social theory: An account of politics, art, and reason based on her psychoanalytic theory.* Chelsea: Bookcrafters, Inc.

Blakemore, E. (2023, July 14). *Barbie's Secret sister was a German novelty doll.* History.com. https://www.history.com/news/barbie-inspiration-bild-lilli

Britannica, T. Editors of Encyclopaedia (2018, March 23). Encyclopedia Britannica. https://www.britannica.com/topic/commission-government.

Cherney, M. A. (2018, April 5). *Mattel CEO makes 4,987 times the typical employee.* MarketWatch. https://www.marketwatch.com/story/mattel-ceo-makes-4987-times-the-typical-employee-2018-04-05

Government of Canada; Crown-Indigenous Relations and Northern Affairs Canada. (2022, September 29). *Truth and reconciliation commission of Canada.* https://www.rcaanc-cirnac.gc.ca/eng/1450124405592/1529106060525

LA Times. (2003, December 23). Mattel wins ruling in barbie dispute. *Los Angeles Times.* Retrieved from https://www.latimes.com/archives/la-xpm-2003-dec-23-fi-barbie23-story.html#:~:text=Greiner%20%26%20Hausser%20collapsed%20in%201983,in%20the%201964%20sale%20agreement

Messina, K. E. (2019). *Misogyny, projective identification, and mentalization: Psychoanalytic, social, and institutional manifestations.* Routledge.

Stewart, E. (2018, April 8). *How does a company's CEO pay compare to its workers? Now you can find out.* Vox. https://www.vox.com/policy-and-politics/2018/4/8/17212796/ceo-pay-ratio-corporate-governance-wealth-inequality

Souli, S. (2020, August 16). *Does America need a truth and reconciliation commission?* Politico. https://www.politico.com/news/magazine/2020/08/16/does-america-need-a-truth-and-reconciliation-commission-395332

Conclusion

Identity formation is a complex element that forms the corpus of a productive, goal-oriented person. It also provides purpose to people based on how they identify with others. *Self-concept* and *self-esteem* also are part of a person's identity. These components involve how we see ourselves as individuals in the context of our families and our communities. Together with identity formation, self-concept and self-esteem allow us to maintain our boundaries as we connect with and relate to others.

After I wrote this book about the identity crisis our country faces through the lens of that quintessential American icon, Barbie, I see this dilemma a little more clearly. As is true with many age-old problems, while I have answered some of the questions that led me to write about identity, more questions have emerged. I think this occurred because I learned the truth about aspects of life in America that were unknown to me; aspects that are not always easy to accept. Following the path of truth and accepting responsibility for wrongdoing strengthens the character of a country, whereas deceit and deception can sap the soul of a nation most of us have learned to love and admire.

I will begin and continue my story—Barbie as a pop-culture icon will endure well beyond the publication of this book—by thinking about Barbie's family and how her relationships as well as her identity were created and maintained throughout the course of her "life." I am proceeding in this manner assuming that she is a person as she was in her analysis versus being a plastic doll. Stay with me. Breathing life into Barbie isn't so crazy—it worked for Greta Gerwig, so I think it works here, too.

While we don't know much about her childhood, we do know she had another identity before she became known in our country as Barbie. We also know she started life fully formed, like a modern-day Galatea, formed not by the sculptor Pygmalion but by toy-making corporations who created their version based on a blond, flirtatious, self-confident secretary. And her first iteration was not one of hard plastic, but as ink on paper, as a sassy Teutonic caricature in German comic strips in 1952. By 1955, her popularity among men (and she was, until then, only considered appropriate for men) had soared; Lilli the doll appeared for sale at German newspaper kiosks as the perfect gag gift for bachelor parties.

Lilli was risqué, sassy, and fun. Always equipped with a quick quip or comeback, *always* fashionably dressed, Lilli had an identity that was all her own. Eventually, German children got ahold of Lilli and a new era of consumerism began.

Eventually, Ruth Handler and her daughter spotted Lilli in a shop in the Swiss Alps while on vacation. They scooped up as many as they could and brought Lilli stateside where she would be reincarnated as Barbie.

With a few minor tweaks, Handler refashioned Lilli into Barbie. Barbie didn't enter the world as Ruth Handler's creation; Lilli's identity was taken from her by the Handlers, who made her their own. Her true identity—her saucy German origins—remained hidden from public view for over 30 years while she was forced to comply with their wishes and desires. Hence, the creation of a fashion doll with many accessories was not original to Ruth Handler, though she claimed credit for the adultlike proportions associated with Barbie.

While Barbie's story is a sad tale of dishonesty and greed, she is a toy. She wasn't kidnapped, murdered, or stoned to death. Far worse crimes are committed on a regular basis in our country multiple times a day. Nevertheless, the way she was taken from the German company that made her was not a highlight of American corporate history.

Lilli's identity was stolen. The Osage Indians lost their identity (and in many cases, their lives) when they lost their mineral rights which made them the richest people per capita in the world. Loss of identity happened to nearly all Indigenous people in North America during the westward expansion. A similar process of erasure occurred with the Black people who lived in the Greenwood area of Tulsa. In this terrible story, racist hatred revealed itself in murderous violence that all but obliterated the collective identity of the inhabitants of Greenwood, America's "Black Wall Street."

Yes, the Barbie story gets dark in this book, but it is necessary so that we may shine a light on what happens when identities disappear or are stolen. There is more at stake than just feeling lost or out of touch. Identity (and lack of it) changes our entire worldview and how we treat each other. This series of essays examines some real-world (and a few imagined ones in Barbie Land) situations where identity was supplanted and what came after.

As the story of *Barbie* the movie continues another, "slap in the face to women" emerged when the Academy Award nominations were announced. Sadly, a majority of the people who made decisions about this year's nominees missed the importance of this movie and of the contributions Margot Robbie and Greta Gerwig have made to one of the biggest problems in our society today: The loss of identity.

Barbie, the blockbuster movie isn't only about plastic dolls, it's about robbing the identity of a person, group of people, or a doll, while replacing it with the robber's own needs. The idea of a fully-figured doll wasn't a toy initially conceived of by Ruth Handler and Mattel that was introduced at the New York Toy Fair in 1959. They stole Bild Lilli, a toy made by a German toy company. It wasn't designed for little girls either, it was made for men's amusement and was often given out as a gag gift at bachelor parties.

Despite protestations to the contrary, it certainly appears as though patriarchy could be involved. Choosing Ryan Gosling over Margot

Robbie and Greta Gerwig doesn't make any sense unless you consider the fact that 67 percent of the voting body of the Academy Awards are male (Statista, 2022).

As Gosling said himself, "But there is no Ken without Barbie, and there is no Barbie movie without Greta Gerwig and Margot Robbie, the two people most responsible for this history-making, globally celebrated film" (Connor, 2024).

REFERENCES

Connor, J. (2024, February8). *Ryan Gosling slams Oscars for failing to nominate Margot Robbie and Greta Gerwig.* TweakTown. https://www.tweaktown.com/news/95813/ryan-gosling-slams-oscars-for-failing-to-nominate-margot-robbie-and-greta-gerwig/index.html

Statista (2022 March). *Distribution of voters of the Academy Awards, by ethnicity.* Statista.com. https://www.statista.com/statistics/321291/voters-academy-awards-ethnicity/#:~:text=Distribution%20of%20voters%20at%20the%20Academy%20Awards%202022%2C%20by%20ethnicity&text=In%202022%2C%20approximately%2081%20percent,the%20Oscars%20voters%20were%20men

About the Author

Dr. Karyne E. Messina is a psychologist and child, adolescent and adult psychoanalyst. In addition to maintaining a full-time private practice in Chevy Chase, Maryland, she is on the medical staff of Suburban Hospital in Bethesda, Maryland which is part of Johns Hopkins Medicine. She is also a podcast host for the New Books Network and chair of the Department of Psychoanalytic Education's (DPE) Scholarship and Writing section which is part of the American Psychoanalytic Association. She has written five books and edited another one that will be available in May. Her topics focus on applying psychoanalytic ideas to real-world problems we all face in our complex world.

www.ingramcontent.com/pod-product-compliance
Lightning Source LLC
Chambersburg PA
CBHW071232020426
42333CB00015B/1440